I0446499

DIGITAL KNOWLEDGE 2024

TRANSFORMATIVE STRATEGIES FOR BUSINESS GROWTH

BY

GRAY S. BERGAN

Copyright

Disclaimer

About The Author

Gray S. Bergan is a leading expert in helping businesses grow using digital knowledge and smart strategies. He knows how to turn complex digital information into simple, practical plans that companies can use to succeed.

Bergan's journey started with a curiosity about data and how it can help businesses. He doesn't just gather information; he finds the important bits that make businesses better. His work isn't just theory; it's about real solutions. Bergan creates easy-to-follow strategies that help businesses turn problems into opportunities, using digital smarts to stay ahead.

Bergan's teachings are like step-by-step guides for success. He shows companies how to adapt, be creative, and use digital insights to grow, even in a fast-changing world. In today's digital world, Gray S. Bergan is a guide, helping businesses make sense of digital tools and strategies, showing them the way to thrive and succeed.

Table of content

INTRODUCTION

In this fast-paced world, you might think, "Why Digital?" Let's keep it simple. Think of the digital domain as a superpower for our daily lives and enterprises. It's not just about gadgets and gizmos; it's about making things easier, faster, and a lot more fun.

Imagine a world where you can connect with anybody, anywhere, in an instant. That's the wonder of turning digital. Whether you're conversing with pals, shopping for excellent things, or conducting a business, the digital revolution is like having a superhero sidekick, making everything more efficient and fun.

So, why should we participate in the digital wave? Well, it's like switching from an outdated flip phone to a super-smart one. The digital world provides a range of opportunities. From sending messages lightning-fast to buying things with a swipe, it's all about making life smoother. But it's not only about great features. Going digital is like having a secret strategy for success.

In this journey, we'll explore why adopting digital isn't simply a choice, it's a prudent step for anyone who wants to succeed in our super-connected society.Think of digital as a toolkit for superheroes. It helps us communicate better, work smarter, and have a blast while doing it. Whether you're a computer specialist or just getting started this introduction is your guide to the "Why" of going digital.

The pulse of connectivity

At its root, the digital revolution is about connectivity. It's the invisible thread running through the fabric of our daily connections, gracefully mending gaps that were once unreachable. Remember the days of

waiting for a letter or the pure anticipation of a phone call? Today, we can share our lives with companions on the opposite side of the earth in an instant. The pulse of connectivity beats powerfully in the digital domain, forging bonds and compressing distances. As technology improves, the pulse gets even colder. Faster connections, better gadgets—it's like a digital upgrade! The future delivers exciting beats, and we get to enjoy the fun. So, the pulse of connectivity is like the heartbeat of our digital world. It's what makes everything quick, engaging, and connected.

Social Fabric of Digital Connectivity

At the heart of the digital experience is social connectivity. Social media platforms have become the modern-day agora, where ideas are shared, communities are built, and voices are amplified. The digital environment isn't just a tool for communication; it's a platform where individuals, businesses, and movements can make their mark on the planet. But with vast reach comes great responsibility. Navigating the social fabric of the digital environment involves a nuanced grasp of online etiquette, ethical sharing, and the ramifications of digital words and deeds. As we communicate in this digital agora, it's vital to develop a culture of respect and empathy. Social media isn't only for fun; it's where we engage with friends, join cool groups, and share our stories. But remember, with huge social power comes great responsibility. It's like being a great friend in this big digital hangout atmosphere.

Chapter 1: The Digital Terrain

To contend in a moment's fast- paced digital request, you must have a thorough understanding of your target audience and marketable openings. To do this, it looks like you must be far and wide as before. Exhausting right? That is, unless you use digital terrain.

Three Reasons To Examine The Terrain

Understanding the position of your HCPs is a good morning point, but digital terrain exploration is the critical tool for staying competitive. There are three satisfying reasons for this:

1. Understand Your Target Audience:

You can challenge and indeed contradict current suppositions by giving quantitative and qualitative validation and perceptivity. You can modify your strategy to fit reality and give more successful engagement possibilities as a result.

2. Discover new possibilities.

Current and unborn trends, similar to new channels, may fill holes in your marketing strategy. An unprejudiced assessment of the competitive terrain identifies areas where contenders fall suddenly, allowing you to act and subsidize those areas.

3. Optimize Investments

Analysis allows you to remodulate investments and optimize spend on channels and means that are most charming to your target audience. Informed opinions grounded on data allow you to spend your budget effectively and constantly boost ROI.

Helping Businesses to comprehend their digital terrain?

A digital terrain is a cooperative name for websites, dispatch, social networks, mobile bias (tablets, smartphones), vids(YouTube), etc. These tools help enterprises vend their products or services. In the world of business there is a smarter and farther nimble contender just around the corner with a superior operation and understanding of technology poised to snare your request.

Understanding your complete digital terrain may insure you are not just keeping an eye on the competition, but that you are also keeping your digital means up to date. We are living in a digital world, nearly everything can be done online(from shopping to banking, to jobs and socializing). further and further our lives depend on digital services.

How can you make sure your business remains at the top?

One simple way of icing your association stays on top is to link your association plan to your IT strategy. A business strategy is the vision for your establishment, the IT strategy is anything connected to technology and how you plan on employing them within your association. It's vital for any successful association to ensure its strategies work in harmony. Aligning business and IT strategies within a pot or association is not a new idea.

Five Important Things to Think About When Connecting IT Strategy with Business:

1. Understand how the business generates income and where it stands in the market.

2. Understand how revenue is impacted by systems and IT

3. Understand client and consumer behavior

4. Acknowledging the value of cost-effectiveness.

5. Adopting a client-centric approach.

Over the last ten years, IT has changed its roles. IT began in the traditional sense (someone with computer knowledge and/or repair skills), and now it encompasses a wide range of roles from web designers, data analysts, digital leaders, cloud specialists, cyber security experts, to repair technicians. There is serious concern in the IT strategy business that there may not be enough skilled workers to cover all the facets of the profession in the near future. People with the right combination of business and IT abilities are scarce in the field of digital leadership.The practice of Managing Directors filling in as Business and IT Managers is hurting smaller firms. A sizable fraction of managing directors lack the time necessary to evaluate strategies, technology, or outcomes.

Digital Marketing

Digital marketing, often known as online marketing, is the establishment of organizations to communicate with implicit visitors via the internet and other forms of digital communication. This includes not only dispatch, social media, and web-based advertising, but also textbook and multimedia dispatches as a marketing channel. In general, digital marketing refers to any marketing problem that involves internet communication. Any form of marketing can help your business thrive. Nonetheless, due to the ease with which digital media may be accessed, digital marketing has become less important. From social media to textbook dispatches, there are numerous ways to employ digital marketing methods in order to engage with your target audience. Additionally, digital marketing has low outspoken costs, making it a cost-effective marketing approach for small businesses.

B2B versus B2C digital marketing

Digital marketing methods work for both B2B (business to business) and B2C (business to consumer) organizations, but style practices range considerably between the two. Here is a closer look at how digital marketing is employed in B2B and B2C marketing strategies. B2B customers have longer decision-making processes and, as a result, longer deal cycles. Relationship-structured methods function better for these guests, but B2C customers respond more to short-term offers and messaging. Professional B2B digital marketers express that B2B transactions are always based on logic and substantiation. B2C content is more likely to be emotionally charged, focusing on making the client feel good about a purchase. B2B transactions typically necessitate more than one person's contribution. The marketing tools that successfully generate these perceptions are participatory and downloadable, whereas B2C visitors prefer one-on-one connections with a business.

Why Digital Marketing Is Important For Business Owners?

Finding the best way to connect and interact with your target audience is one of the hardest aspects of running a business, regardless of how long you've been in operation. If you can't reach the appropriate audience at the right moment, no amount of flawless product creation or very effective logistics will help.

How much do you know about digital marketing? You know about billboards, magazines, commercials, and other conventional types of promotion. Pop-ups and banner adverts on websites are probably what many company executives think of. Some know that an essential component of digital marketing is having a well-maintained social media presence. Though you may be familiar with some of the strategies used in digital marketing, what distinguishes successful digital advertisements from more conventional ones?

Reaching a More Targeted Audience: When you buy an advertisement in a print publication, the people who see it are the subscribers to your newspaper. When you acquire a time slot, your audience is the people that tune in to that TV station particularly to watch that show at that time. Conventional media often does not let you tailor your message for certain groups, even while some demographic distinctions may be established based on the medium (for instance, subscribers of Golf magazine are probably golf fans). Everyone has to buy food, but how do advertisements affect people in different age groups, like 18 and 55?

Digital marketing platforms provide you the freedom to target people based on a variety of criteria, like age, gender, income, geography, occupation, hobbies, and more, all at no extra cost. Furthermore, free analytics tools linked to websites like Google and Facebook provide you precise information on the demographics of page followers and website visitors, even if you're not sure which breakdown relates to your business.

Brand Recognition: Whenever you use traditional advertising to promote your brand, a new product, or a service, you are depending on the likelihood that your target market will be able to notice your efforts. Mostly, you have to rely on individuals showing up at the appropriate place at the appropriate time, whether it's a person glancing at your booth's brochure or someone driving the proper route to work. However, the vast majority of clients utilize the internet sometimes throughout the day. Digital marketing platforms allow you to reach your audience whenever they check their smartphone or PC. If you want to target a certain customer segment with a particular product or aspect of your company, you may also accomplish so.

Creating Leads:

Measuring your performance is one of the main problems with conventional marketing. The number of individuals who viewed your commercial may be precisely known to media buyers, but how can you demonstrate that it resulted in a sale?You may run digital advertisements and include forms for contact information. It does three things for you: it informs you how many people clicked on the advertisement and interacted with it in the manner you intended; it allows you to add those individuals to your phone and email lists; and last, it provides you with an instant chance to qualify the lead. In order to turn a lead into a sale, that prompt reaction is crucial.

Interaction and Retention of Customers:

Maintaining customer engagement is a major business function for pubs and restaurants, therefore it's not difficult to do. Still, how can a small-batch distillery communicate with a customer who lives 2,000 miles away from them?

With the use of social media postings, email newsletters, and review management, business owners can interact with their consumers in many ways thanks to technology. Digital channels allow you to address a customer's bad review in a public setting, so not only can you address their issues, but your answer will also be visible to each and every reader of the review. You may also create a devoted online community around your business by interacting with clients who have had good experiences with you.

Keep Your Customers Informed:

It's still possible to reach a large audience using traditional marketing. Yet nothing is more successful than digital marketing if you want to really interact with your audience and find out what messages they react to.

Understanding the Role of a Digital Marketer:

Understanding the role and responsibilities of a digital marketer is essential before diving into the field of digital marketing. A digital marketer is in charge of developing, implementing, and maintaining online marketing campaigns in order to promote a brand, product, or service. They use social media, search engines, email marketing, content marketing, and other digital platforms to raise brand awareness, generate leads, and increase sales. To stay ahead of the competition, you must keep up with the latest trends, technologies, and approaches in the sector as a digital marketer.

Core Skill Development:

To thrive as a digital marketer, you must cultivate a set of core skills that will set you apart from the competition. These abilities include the following:

a. Analytical Skills: Analyzing data, identifying patterns, and making data-driven decisions are all part of digital marketing. Developing strong analytical skills will enable you to assess the success of your marketing efforts and make necessary changes for better results.

b. Innovative Thinking: Out-of-the-box thinking and innovation are frequently required in digital marketing. Developing a creative mindset can assist you in developing one-of-a-kind marketing tactics and intriguing content that will appeal to your target audience.

c. Technical Ability: Dealing with multiple tools, platforms, and technologies is part of digital marketing. It is critical for success in this field to have a solid technical understanding of website optimization, SEO, social networking platforms, content management systems, and analytics tools.

d. Collaboration and Communication Skills: Because digital marketing is a collaborative business, it necessitates effective communication with a wide range of stakeholders, including clients, designers, developers, and content creators. Strong communication skills can assist you in successfully explaining your ideas and executing marketing activities.

Getting started in digital marketing without any prior expertise:

Skills in digital marketing are in high demand in the present climate. Thus, in the event that you lack experience, you may be unsure of where to begin. Relax, no prior experience is required to become a digital marketer. Understanding these fundamentals , ideas, and

procedures are crucial for digital marketing. To make it happen, do these steps:

1. Find Your Area of Interest Specialization:

Within the vast realm of internet marketing, you have the option to concentrate on everything from

a. SEO stands for search engine optimization.

b. Pay-per-click (PPC) advertising via social media using email as a marketing tool Promoting content.

As these areas are crucial to a company's overall marketing plan, choose a digital marketing specialization that you are enthusiastic and interested in.

2. Expand Your Basic Knowledge Base:

Digital marketers need to make sure they are well-versed in the concepts and best practices of digital advertising. Increasing your basic knowledge may be achieved by reading thought-provoking blog entries, seeing YouTube videos, looking through Reddit threads, and using other free resources, like this SEO best practices guide.

Use Google Analytics or another analytics tool, for instance, to brush up on your data analytics knowledge if you're a beginner content marketer. In addition to learning about social media measurement tools like Hootsuite or Sprout Social, you should concentrate on social media marketing.

3. Become Certified or Enroll in a Course:

Getting a professional credential or enrolling in an online course might be a good idea if you want to learn more about the subject of digital marketing. One may get practical experience with the newest technology and study the principles of digital marketing with this fantastic method.

4. Create a Portfolio for Digital Marketing.

Once you've grasped the ideas thoroughly, it's time to put your expertise in digital marketing to the test. Creating a genuine marketing campaign portfolio to present to prospective companies is the best method to do this.

Because PPC advertising platforms provide quickly and readily measurable results, it's a wonderful idea to start by looking at Google Ads or Facebook Ads. This will demonstrate to prospective employers that you are familiar with the principles of digital marketing in addition to providing you with vital information about your skill set.

5. Build an offline and online network: Make sure you're connecting with other offline and online digital marketing experts in order to get your first job. Digital marketing specialists may be found on social media sites such as Facebook, LinkedIn, and Twitter.

Meeting people at meetings and conferences for digital marketing is also beneficial. These are fantastic chances to network with more seasoned workers, meet new ones, and break into the IT business.

6. Apply for work in both in-house and agency settings: This is a smart strategy for breaking into the digital marketing sector. Building your portfolio and earning significant work experience are just two of the many benefits of working for a digital marketing business.

7. Look for Similar Employment to Open Doors: Seeking for similar jobs that can expand your resume and assist in the development of your technical abilities is another method to get experience as a digitizer.

Among the related occupations are the following:

a. specialist in content marketing and a technician for sales representatives

b. Social media manager and consultant for digital marketing

c. creators of content

d. data analysts

e. UI/UX designers

f. logo and brand designers

Gaining insightful knowledge and soft skills that you may use to a digital marketing position can be achieved in any of these vocations.

8. Use Reasonably Priced Freelancing to Gain Experience in the Work Field: Hiring remote jobs in digital marketing is made simple by job boards and inexpensive freelance platforms like Upwork and Fiverr. This is not advised, but as a temporary fix, it may be a terrific way to expand your clientele and cultivate partnerships.

Digitized Tools

To enhance your marketing strategy and return on investment, as a digital marketer, you need to familiarize yourself with the many technologies at your disposal. Digital marketing technologies will enable you to implement the right plans in the right way. These tools are meant to support your organizational efforts while enabling you to make adjustments as necessary.

To enhance your marketing strategy and return on investment, as a digital marketer, you need to familiarize yourself with the many technologies at your disposal. Digital marketing technologies will enable you to implement the right plans in the right way. These tools are meant to support your organizational efforts while enabling you to make adjustments as necessary.

1. Mailchimp

MailChimp is an email marketing and social advertising solution that simplifies the planning and automation of digital marketing campaigns. It's one of the best digital marketing tools accessible for creating campaigns and tracking visitors. The platform also has other connections that it supports with other SaaS providers. The technologies used in email marketing may help you establish a strong connection with your audience. MailChimp is one well-known provider of email marketing.

The following are a few of MailChimp's features:

1. Content is improved via the use of simple design concepts.

2. Make unique designs with the aid of an AI-powered assistant.

3. You may create personalized emails and get up to six times as many transactions by using automation.

4. provides techniques for gathering data and insights in one location.

5. Provide a free plan to small shops as well.

6. You may communicate with the appropriate individuals at the appropriate time by using MailChimp's pre-built, personalized email automation. The greatest part is that you can use automated welcome messages, order notifications, and happy birthday messages to stay at the top of your customers' thoughts.

7. With MailChimp's assistance, online retailers and e-commerce companies may increase traffic, income, and conversions.

2. Analytic Google

One powerful tool for digital marketing that could help you with a range of marketing decisions is Google Analytics. You can easily track your e-commerce business and goals to keep your company on track. With the help of the different data insights provided by Google Analytics, marketers can have a better understanding of the procedures that must be followed while making changes and enhancements to their websites. To begin going, all you have to do is install Google Analytics on your website.

One of Google Analytics' advantages

1. Is the provision of segmented statistics on website visitors based on devices, items, pages, and other variables.

2. Make your own dashboards, dimensions, and metrics for quick access to data and insights.

3. It could help you comprehend your target audience more clearly.

4. You'll receive real-time information on who is visiting your website and what pages they are currently viewing.

5. Making your landing page more intuitive for your clients could help you make it more engaging.

6. Permit you to get a sense of how the company functions.

7. Permit you to use many reporting formats to share your findings.

8. Enable data to be arranged and displayed for business use

Google Marketing

Regardless of size, nearly any business can benefit from Google AdWords. Even though a lot of marketers think Google AdWords is too expensive, it's one of the most powerful digital marketing tools available and might propel your business to new heights.

The following features are included in Google Ads:

1. You could get more calls from clients if you included a click-to-call button.

2. Boost the quantity of customers that come into your stores.

3. One of the greatest things about Google Ads is how easy it is to figure out the ROI.

4. Additionally, the website is significantly faster and easier to use thanks to new artificial intelligence features. You might see faster results with display advertising thanks to its AI components.

5. You can target your customer base based on a number of variables, including career, geography, age, and gender. Other digital marketing platforms don't have this feature.

6. Most importantly, if you want to know about the newest Google services, you can visit Google Agency Account Strategist. 7. Additionally, it provides access to certain beta testing.

8. Your surveys are simple to use, well-designed, and responsive to mobile devices.

4. Canva Enterprise

If you work in digital marketing, you are aware of the necessity for a high-quality design tool that can assist you in creating exceptional content for social media and other marketing purposes. Canva is a well-known design platform that assists you in creating effective marketing campaigns with graphic content that you can post on your websites, blogs, social media accounts, and other channels. The foundation of any digital marketing campaign is visual material. You must create blogs that are visually appealing in order to draw in the target group of customers.

Canva's features include:

1. You can modify posts and make graphs of any kind using Canva.
2. The utility has multiple templates in it.

3. You can use its extensive library of stock pictures, graphics, icons, vectors, and images to create any kind of visual content for your marketing campaign.

4. You can select from an extensive range of designs, including those for postcards, brochures, CD covers, wallpaper, books, resumes, certificates, magazine covers, letterheads, blog banners, presentations, logos, and social media.

5. Its easy-to-use drag-and-drop interface lets you create visual elements that match your campaign. 6.The best part is that creating graphic content for your digital marketing campaign doesn't require the services of a professional designer.

7. Anyone without any experience in design can use it because it is that simple.

5. Microsoft Trello

Trello is a viable option if you're looking for a content management system that may assist you in ideating and planning content for your digital marketing plan. For the purpose of creating, organizing, and scheduling online content, hundreds of thousands of digital marketers employ one of the most well-liked content management systems on the planet.

The team is kept together by the software, which facilitates and controls communication. To allow team members to collaborate on a project, you can put many team members on a single card. In this manner, you will be aware of who is responsible for creating, crafting, revising, publishing, and tagging calls to action inside a post.

The features of Trello include:

1. lets you create cards, include notes about the card's subject, set deadlines, and designate themes to particular teams.

2. makes it possible for your teams to operate remotely and access their assignments and projects from any location.

6. Slack

Every day, digital marketers make use of Slack. Slack allows you to share pertinent content, send messages, and talk about client work, new articles, projects, and support issues.

In the event that your workforce consists of digital marketers, you will require a potent method of effectively communicating with them. Here's when Slack becomes useful.

Slack's features include:

1. simplifies real-time online communication among team members.

2. Permit you to follow any content associated with the teams, projects, and channels.

3. Let you use video conferencing and messaging as well.

4. Help teams work together from any location.

5. Despite its seeming simplicity, this software is much more than just a texting app. You may be able to increase the effectiveness of your organization with slack.

6. It isn't a tool for project management or collaboration. It functions as a chat app with a large number of settings and options.

8. You can hold public, searchable group conversations with it, even private ones.

9. You can make new groups and change the interface's color scheme.

7. Yoast SEO

Yoast SEO is undoubtedly familiar to you. One of the most popular and widely used WordPress plugins for digital marketers to optimize their websites for better search engine rankings is this one.

Yoast SEO assists with the specifics that WordPress is not very good at: creating content, using webmaster tools, submitting sitemaps, and so forth.

Yoast SEO's features include:

There are several features in the program that help you make your website better.

1. Includes capabilities to handle duplicate content, rich snippets, XML sitemaps, meta keywords, description management, and built-in content analysis.

2. Enables you to produce content for your digital marketing campaigns that is more effective.

3. With the help of the plugin, you can create a meta description and meta title for your content in the Yoast SEO meta box.

4. Furthermore, installing a third-party plugin for XML sitemaps is not necessary. It creates XML sitemaps for websites automatically and submits them to search engines.

The best aspect is that you can protect your RSS feed from content scrapers and plagiarism. This keeps other websites from stealing your work and posting it under your name.

8. Survey Anyplace

Examine The best platform for marketers to create engaging and interactive tests, assessments, and questionnaires for their target audience is Anyplace. It's a fantastic digital marketing tool that will help you interact with your target market and build personality and brand recognition.

You may use this tool to create high-quality surveys for your digital marketing campaigns that will benefit you in the long run if you're tired of using traditional surveys to find out what the market is now looking for in terms of a product or business.

Survey Anyplace's features include:

1.Enables you to create tests that provide insightful information.

2.Gives specific advice in response to the respondents.

3.Aids in comprehending consumer expectations, what characteristics they are looking for, what the market is expecting, and more.

4.You may create your own brand and have your branding appear on surveys and quizzes using SurveyAnyplace. Simply put, you may build a brand that meets the expectations of your customers based on the user experience.

5.The finest feature of the platform is that it lets you create custom survey questions and includes photo options.

9. Ahrefs

With the help of Ahrefs' suite of SEO tools, you can easily improve your website in accordance with your marketing goals. With its massive data index, the tool is undoubtedly one of the most sought-after digital marketing tools available today. It is usually used for backlink verification.

The attributes of Ahrefs

1.Permit you to improve your website.

2.Let you select the appropriate websites for your material and choose topics wisely.

3.It's a comprehensive SaaS platform with data index, testimonial snippets, and a free trial available.

4.Give your projects to you to manage.

5.let you monitor the advancement of your ranking.

10. SEMURUSH

With the use of SEO, content marketing, market research, advertising, social media management, and search engine reputation management, SEMRUSH is an all-in-one marketing toolbox that helps increase a company's online visibility.

SEMRUSH's attributes include:

1.Uses SEO tools and procedures to improve organic traffic.

2.support the creation of material that is ranked.

3.reveals the strategies and techniques used by rivals

4.Aids in the identification of tactics for reaching out to more prospects while spending less money.

5.helps with the development of social media plans.

11. Loomly

Users may plan, create, and publish content across several platforms with the aid of Loomly, a digital marketing calendar and social media management tool. It features a post preview feature to see how material will look across various platforms, a content library to store and organize assets, and a calendar view for scheduling articles. It also comes with data to monitor engagement and performance as well as collaborative tools.Simple, easy-to-use consumers who may not be the most tech-savvy will find the interface inviting and easy to use. The cost of the platform is appealing to solopreneurs and small businesses who want to take control of their social media profile.

12. Audeinse

Audiense is a platform for audience intelligence and social media analytics. It was formerly known as SocialBro. It provides information on social media users' demographics, interests, and activity, along with statistics. It lets you identify key influencers by analyzing both your own and your competitors' social media followings. Moreover, it provides possibilities for targeting, segmentation, and interaction, including the ability to create custom audience segments and send direct messages that are sent automatically. To better understand and interact with their social media audience and advance their social media strategy, companies, agencies, and marketers use it.

13. Hubspot

With the help of Hubspot, businesses can create, manage, and optimize the content for their websites and blogs. Hubspot also includes a marketing automation tool and a CRM (customer relationship management) system. It also provides email marketing, reporting, analytics, and social media management features. Along with several paid variants with additional features and capabilities, there is a free version as well.

14. Lemlist

Lemlist is an email outreach automation platform that aids businesses in expanding their marketing and sales efforts that reach out to customers. Customers may use information like the recipient's name, company, and more to automatically embed bespoke images and videos into emails, allowing them to personalize their email campaigns at scale. Numerous features are also available, including lead scoring, email tracking, and automated follow-ups. Sales, marketing, and business development teams use Lemlist extensively to improve response rates, personalize communications, and automate outreach processes.

15. The Clearscope

Natural language processing (NLP) and machine learning are used by the content optimization platform Clearscope to assess and improve the content for readability and search engine optimization. In addition to assisting users in locating and optimizing for the most pertinent words, phrases, and topics in their content, it also helps them detect and fix any readability, grammar, and style issues. To enhance the effectiveness of their online content and boost organic traffic, copywriters, SEO specialists, and content marketers use Clearscope extensively. It may be combined with a variety of content management systems (CMS), including Hubspot, WordPress, and others.

16. Relache

With the use of landing page and website optimization software like Unbounce, companies can design, publish, and test pop-ups, sticky bars, and landing pages without having to hire web developers or IT staff. It comes with pre-designed themes and a visual editor that lets users create custom pop-ups and landing pages. A/B testing, conversion statistics, dynamic text replacement, and integration with other marketing tools like email service providers, CRMs, and more are among the features it offers. To improve conversion rates, generate leads, and increase sales, digital marketers, advertisers, and companies use Unbounce extensively.

17. Optimizely

Optimizely is a landing page testing platform that combines audience targeting and graphic design capabilities to quickly test various audience segments. Enhancing the performance of your website doesn't have to be difficult if you use a no-code platform. You can test both major and minor changes to your pages.

18. Clearbit

Clearbit is a data and API provider that gives businesses access to both individual and commercial consumer information. It offers many services, including:

1.Clearbit offers data about businesses, similar to their position, size, technology mound, and other specifics.

2.Enrichment, Clearbit can enhance an association's being a client database with redundant data, similar to technographics and firmographics.

3.Lead generation, Clearbit can help associations induce new leads by finding and vetting new implicit consumers.

4.Threat operation, Clearbit can help enterprises decry and reduce fraudulent exertion by offering data on companies and individualities.

19. Typeform

With Typeform, an online platform for making forms and checks, druggies can produce and partake dynamic and engaging forms, checks, and quizzes. It features several malleable themes and design possibilities, as well as an intuitive drag- and- drop interface. It also has capabilities like tentative sense, data confirmation, and real- time analytics. Typeform can be used for numerous different effects, similar as gathering feedback, registering events, conducting exploration, and generating leads. It may be combined with other apps similar as Google wastes, Salesforce, Mailchimp, and more.

20. Visme

The pall- grounded visual content product platform Visme allows druggies to produce and edit a wide range of visual content, similar as infographics, donations, social media plates, and more. With a drag- and- drop editor and a large collection of design templates, druggies may produce and alter their own designs. Also, a library of stock prints, icons, and plates are available. Visme also offers tools for interactive factors, vitality, and data visualization. druggies can post and distribute their material on multitudinous websites, blogs, and social media platforms. It's extensively used by marketers, preceptors, and commercial directors to give aesthetically pleasing content that effectively conveys generalities and information. These tools will help you understand and manage your digital marketing enterprise more successfully. Be advised that all of them demand payment, indeed though some offer a free trial. Still, the cost is warranted.

What's a digital marketing strategy?

A digital marketing strategy is a plan that describes how your business will create an online presence on several platforms. The last phase in a marketing strategy to attract more clients who meet your target demographic and convince them to become paying guests is to increase your online presence. Different approaches and methods for marketing Whilst researching digital marketing, you may want to check up the terms "selling strategy" and "marketing approach". So what distinguishes them from one other? A well considered plan outlining how you will use Internet marketing to disprove your claims is called a marketing strategy.

A marketing strategy is a specific plan of action that you will use to reach your objective. Examples of common marketing tactics include writing articles and blogs, sending emails to implied visitors, and running adverts. Strategies opposing marketing behemoths When you are organizing your strategy, you can hear the term "marketing crusade". Now let's discuss how it differs from a digital marketing strategy. It was previously said that a marketing plan is the blueprint outlining how you will interact with and persuade your target audience to become online purchasers. It sets out your whole marketing and business pretense. Instead of focusing on your end objective, a marketing campaign is an advertising campaign created to assist you with negotiating a certain approach. For juggernauts, there are often start and completion dates. For example, you might begin running a string of Google advertisements to drive more revenue over the course of four months.

Chapter 2: Types of Digital Marketing Strategies

1. Search machine optimization(SEO)

Search engines are a major source of information for consumers in the digital era since there is a wealth of information available.

According to research, the vast majority of clicks occur on the first few results that appear on a search engine results page (SERP). That being said, having your website buried on page three or higher is like having a great book stashed away in the basement of the library, where very few will ever find it.

Better user experiences are the main goal of SEO, not merely rankings. Your website will become more useful, comprehensible, and accessible to search engines and people if it is optimized.

The process of improving a website's exposure on search engines like Google, Bing, or Yahoo is known as SEO, or search engine optimization. Increasing the likelihood that your website will show up in the top results when someone searches for relevant keywords or phrases is the aim.

Think of search engines as the librarians and the internet as a huge library. A search engine searches its index when you put a query into it to get the most relevant and helpful results. Search engine optimization (SEO) is similar to structuring your book so that a search engine, or library, can locate it easily when someone is seeking for relevant subjects.

Why employ SEO?

Think of SEO as a demand for your digital marketing plan. No matter where they're in your buying channel, it catches every member of your target followership. The logic behind this is because nearly all druggies start their hunt for a new goods or service on a hunt machine. For example, did you know that eighty percent of consumers conduct online product exploration? Or that over half of consumers find a new product or company after conducting a hunt. It might be your business if you use SEO as one of your internet marketing strategies.

2. Pay-per-click (PPC) advertising

PPC advertising is a type of advertising sponsorship that operates on an auction basis.

Pay Per Click (PPC) advertising involves bidding on the keywords you want to show up for. It will only display your advertisement when someone searches for those terms. These adverts then show up at the top of search results, above the organic listings. If a user decides to click on one of your adverts, you will then have to pay. Stated differently, the only cost is the outcome and not the advertising space. PPC aims to attract transactional queries, or searchers who are ready to make a purchase. After clicking on your advertisement, they will be directed to your landing page where they will see a call-to-action (CTA) encouraging them to convert by making a purchase, signing up for an email subscription, or doing something else.

Why even use PPC?

Pay-per-click advertising is among the most affordable kinds of commercial advertising. For a lot of organizations who are either new to digital marketing or need a quick boost, PPC advertising is a great online marketing technique. Pay-Per-Click (PPC) advertising is chosen by companies for a number of reasons:

1. Quick results: PPC advertisements have the ability to send visitors to a website or landing page in a matter of seconds. PPC may provide traffic and possible leads right away, in contrast to other marketing techniques like SEO, which may take months to produce results.

2. Focused audience: Pay-per-click advertising enables companies to target certain areas, demographics, and hobbies. By selecting keywords and crafting advertising according to the traits of their target demographic, advertisers can make sure the correct people see their message.

3. Cost control: Businesses using Pay Per Click (PPC) may establish a budget and only pay when a user clicks on their advertisement. As a result, you have financial control and can limit your investment to advertising that really increases engagement.

4.Detailed analytics and statistics on ad success are provided by PPC systems, resulting in quantifiable outcomes. This enables companies to monitor conversions, precisely track their return on investment (ROI), and make the required modifications to maximize the efficacy of their campaigns.

5. Brand exposure: Pay-per-click advertisements may raise brand recognition and visibility. Users may help with brand awareness and recall even if they choose not to click on the advertisements.

6. Competitive advantage: PPC advertising gives companies an advantage over their rivals by focusing on terms and phrases that they may not be focusing on. By

doing this, you may draw in more attention and possible clients who are looking for those particular keywords.

3. Content-based marketing

Using content to connect, engage, and reach customers is the aim of content marketing for your business. This information, which may include blog entries, infographics, videos, and more, can be beneficial to users. For example, if your business sells ski and snowboard equipment, you could write an article detailing what a beginner needs for their first outing. You may also create articles about how to maintain a snowboard and what accessories can aid enhance ski performance. The primary objectives of content marketing, as a digital media strategy, are to increase traffic, produce leads, and offer

relevant information to your target audience. In a technical sense, content marketing also focuses on optimizing your content for search engines to make it more visible.

Why use content-based marketing?

Businesses and marketers use content-based marketing for a variety of reasons, such as:

1.Businesses may establish themselves as industry thought leaders by producing and disseminating the greatest educational resources. Their target audience gains credibility and trust as a result.

2. Creating leads: Businesses may use content to attract and involve prospective clients, convincing them to download a whitepaper, sign up for a newsletter, or make a purchase.

3. Raising brand awareness: By using content marketing, companies may expose themselves to a larger audience and get more visibility. It's possible that they may improve brand recall and awareness by producing excellent content.

4. Boosting client loyalty and engagement: Companies that regularly provide insightful and relevant content may maintain audience interest and participation. Increased client loyalty and repeat business might result from this.

5. Customer education: Customers may learn about goods, services, or developments in the sector via content-based marketing. This facilitates decision-making for clients and establishes the company as a reliable source.

6. Setting yourself apart from rivals: Using content-based marketing, companies may make a name for themselves in a congested industry. Businesses may draw in and hold the interest of their intended audience by providing them with interesting and worthwhile information.

4. Email promotions

Email marketing is an internet marketing technique that involves promoting your products and services to your target market, cultivating email leads, and strengthening brand loyalty.

The dual objectives of email marketing are attracting new clients and retaining existing ones. It's a great tactic to increase customer awareness of your brand, foster repeat business, and sustain brand recognition.

The idea is that these clients will remember you for future purchases even if they don't now need your products or services. People are motivated to choose your firm because of its brand awareness when they're ready to buy.

As a digital marketing approach, email marketing's primary objective is to stay in front of potential customers' eyes and to keep current clients coming back with educational materials like product coupons and news that is pertinent to the sector.

Why Use Email Marketing?

In this sense, email marketing is very advantageous. Because of this, over 80% of businesses, including technology firms, retail stores, and manufacturing industries, use email marketing.

Email marketing is used by organizations for a variety of reasons:

1. Economical: Reaching a big audience at a low cost may be achieved via email marketing. Emailing someone is often less expensive than utilizing a more conventional approach, like direct mail.

2. Direct communication: Businesses may speak with their audience directly using email. It's a personal, customized kind of communication that may be made for certain people or organizations.

3. Targeted messaging: Companies may use email marketing to divide and focus on certain audiences according to their interests, demographics, or past exchanges. Sending messages that are more relevant and tailored is now possible.

4. Measurable outcomes: Email marketing yields numerical outcomes. Companies may monitor key performance indicators (KPIs) like conversions, open rates, and click-through rates to assess how successful their campaigns are.

5. Automation: Email marketing systems sometimes come with automation features that let companies create campaigns that start on their own when certain conditions are satisfied. Businesses may save time and effort by doing this and yet maintain continual contact with their audience.

6. Greater brand awareness and client loyalty: Regular email marketing helps clients remember the business and increases brand recognition. Additionally, by offering updates, discounts, or useful information, it fosters client loyalty.

7. Easy to forward and share: Email users may forward or share content with ease, which can help companies expand their clientele via word-of-mouth advertising.

8. Integration with other marketing channels: By combining email marketing with other marketing channels like social media or content marketing, you can provide clients a unified and consistent brand experience.

5. Social media promotion

Increasing conversions and brand recognition are social media marketing's primary objectives. In a social media marketing strategy, one or more of the following social media platform types may be used: LinkedIn, Pinterest, Instagram, Twitter, and Facebook. In addition to social media brand marketing, this strategy typically involves advertising.

Why do people use social media?

While less than 30% of firms use social media as a marketing strategy, there is a big opportunity for those that invest in the platform. Even better, social media makes up about 25% of users' online time, proving that it's a highly effective means of communication.

Social media use is motivated by a variety of factors, including:

1. Establishing connections: Users may stay in touch with friends, family, and acquaintances by using social media. It provides a user-friendly interface for communicating and sustaining relationships.

2. Information sharing: Users may shed light on their lives and hobbies by providing their network with updates, photos, videos, and other content.

3. Networking: Through social media platforms, employees may connect with coworkers, clients, and peers in similar fields. People might use it to expand their professional networks and hunt for employment opportunities.

4. Entertainment: Sports highlights, funny videos, memes, and other entertaining content may all be found on social media. Fans of brands, influencers, and celebrities may be followed to stay up to date on their actions.

5. Information and news: Many people use social media to get news and information about news, fascinating topics, and current events. It provides a forum for inter-source information sharing and discovery.

6. Helping others and exchanging first-hand information on topics like relationships, health, and hobbies: Social media creates a sense of community and may be used as a platform for people to ask for help, provide advice, or both.

7. Promoting companies: Businesses and entrepreneurs advertise their brands, products, and services via social media. Both advertising options and a way to interact with potential customers are offered.

8. Social media provides a forum for users to express themselves creatively and via their own artwork, photographs, messages, and other mediums. It provides room for individuality and artistic expression.

9.Social media is a tool that people use to discover new ideas and trends as well as sources of inspiration. It may be an inspiration and source of information in many other disciplines, such as fashion, travel, culinary arts, and more.

10. Developing a sense of community: By joining groups, communities, or fan sites, social media users may establish connections with others who share their interests, hobbies, or worries. Along with fostering a sense of camaraderie and community, it facilitates connections between like-minded individuals.

6. An improvement to voice search

With voice search optimization, your business may make both new and existing website content more voice search friendly. Having your website show up as the highlighted snippet or at position zero in Google search results is the aim. Because search queries differ when completed by speech vs text, voice search optimization is crucial. This is particularly crucial if you own a local business, as many consumers regularly use voice search on their mobile devices to locate a hardware store, restaurant, or hair salon in their area.

Why do people use voice search Optimization?

Voice search optimization is used by people for several purposes:

1.Convenience: Voice search enables hands-free searching, which makes it ideal for multitasking, cooking, and driving.

2. Speed and efficiency: Users may locate information more quickly and effectively by using voice search since it is often quicker than typing, particularly for lengthier searches.

3. Accessibility: For those who have trouble typing or who have physical limitations, voice search provides an accessible option.

4.Natural language inquiries: Instead of needing to modify their vocabulary to suit conventional written searches, voice search enables users to talk spontaneously, using whole phrases or questions.

5. Local search intent: Since voice search offers more relevant results depending on the user's location, it is often used for local inquiries like locating nearby eateries, stores, or services.

6.Increasing popularity of speech-enabled devices: Making your content voice search friendly guarantees exposure and discoverability on voice-enabled devices, such as smart speakers and virtual assistants like Google Assistant, Alexa, or Siri.

7. Viral advertising

Your business broadens its customer base, boosts income, and flourishes thanks to video marketing. Similar to email marketing and content marketing, your company concentrates on producing educational and worthwhile videos for its intended audience.

Why do people employ viral advertising?

A business or brand may decide to employ viral advertising for a number of reasons, including:

1. Enhanced brand exposure: Viral advertising has the power to quickly reach a huge audience. A campaign's potential to go viral may result in substantial exposure for the company, raising its profile and recognition.

2. Economical: When considering marketing strategies, viral advertising may be less expensive than conventional techniques. The process of starting a viral campaign often includes producing interesting and shareable content that may increase organic reach and reduce advertising expenses.

3. Increased brand engagement: Viral ads often have a strong hook and fascinating quality that raises brand awareness. Content that appeals to people is more likely to be interacted with and shared, which enables companies to build stronger bonds with their target market.

4. Targeted reach: Viral marketing may be able to more successfully reach a certain target audience than conventional advertising. Brands may raise the possibility that their message will be spread within a community by producing content that appeals to a certain demographic or set of people.

5. Making the most of social media power: Social media platforms are a major source of viral advertising as people there often share and interact with information. Brands may take use of the network effect, which is the quick dissemination of information across many user networks, to extend their reach by using social media platforms.

6. Possibility for originality and creativity: Creating distinctive, imaginative material that sticks out from the crowd is often required for viral advertising. Brands may be able to use this as a chance to demonstrate their ingenuity and inventiveness while developing an unforgettable and significant campaign.

7. Making advantage of user-generated content: Social media campaigns that go viral often inspire people to participate and provide material that they have created. This not only increases interaction but also gives businesses access to excellent user-generated material that they can use for other marketing campaigns.

Data's Event-Based Use in Digital Marketing:

Businesses can better understand their consumers, anticipate consumer trends, and increase the return on investment of their marketing initiatives by utilizing data in digital marketing. It can also assist a company in monitoring the consumer journey. A business may more readily connect with clients at various points in the purchasing process when it has a deeper understanding of the customer journey. Digital marketers can enhance their ability to identify objectives and market a company's services to specific consumers by employing data analysis, which is the act of gathering and evaluating data to obtain insights. Metrics pertaining to social media, content on websites and blogs, email marketing, online adverts, and mobile downloads are examples of data in digital marketing. Effective utilization of this data by marketers allows them to obtain insights into methods that increase the performance of their digital initiatives.

Advantages of Data-Driven Digital Marketing

Data can be used by digital marketers to better understand their target markets and effectively promote a company's goods or services. For these workers, gathering, evaluating, and assessing various forms of data can be quite advantageous. In particular, the following facts can benefit digital marketers:

1.Recognize customers: Employees in digital marketing might utilize data to gather facts to comprehend both present and prospective customers for their firm. They can reach audiences with focused marketing efforts by using data to examine customer demographics, interests, and purchase patterns.

Through audience-specific service targeting, businesses can provide a customized user experience that can enhance customer satisfaction. Additionally, by getting to know their clientele, digital marketers may better target their campaigns and collaborate with product teams to develop offers that satisfy their target audience. This can increase client loyalty and aid digital marketers in keeping customers.

2.Find new opportunities: A common practice among digital marketers is to routinely analyze data in order to spot trends that may eventually lead to the discovery of new chances. For instance, they might look at internet activity to find chances to market a new product to both current and potential clients.

3.Create a customized experience: Using data, digital marketers can use marketing campaigns to give clients a customized experience. For instance, they can utilize data to pinpoint the target market for a fresh campaign and provide content tailored to that particular demographic. Increased consumer involvement from this strategy may contribute to a rise in conversions.

4.Boost marketing results:

These workers evaluate marketing campaign data to ascertain the efficacy of various tactics, including social media posts and online ads. They can increase their marketing results by utilizing this information to modify upcoming initiatives.

5.Increase brand recognition:

A corporation can identify the most successful promotional and advertising techniques by reviewing pertinent data. They can put these tactics into practice to choose the best channels to leverage in order to build brand awareness and connect with the right target audiences.

6.Real-time consumer access:

By combining data with automated solutions, a digital marketer may connect with clients at the exact moment when they are actively considering making a purchase. Within an organization's email marketing platform, for instance, a digital marketer can integrate social media activity, website visits, purchase habits, and other data. Subsequently, email campaigns can be initiated to target people at the optimal moment for them to open and interact with the brand.

Data-driven strategies for digital marketing:

A variety of data can be used by digital marketers to track and enhance their marketing initiatives. Various forms of data can be utilized in digital marketing in the following ways:

1. Internet data :

Data can be used to comprehend user behavior on a business website. These website statistics can be gathered and measured with the use of a variety of analytics tools. These tools can give information about the geographical and age ranges of website viewers. Analyzing website data can assist you in comprehending how visitors arrive at the site and the pages they browse while there.

Website data, for instance, may reveal that a user accessed the website by clicking on a social network post, after which they visited two other URLs. Knowing how consumers arrived at a business's website can help you with your digital marketing plan.

2. Social media data:

You may examine a company's social media followers and see how they interact with content by using this kind of data. Social media networks have built-in tools or third-party applications that you may use to track social media analytics. Various data, including the

demographics of followers and the quantity of people who interact with a post, can be obtained from these analytics.

With this data, you may efficiently target various audiences and spot patterns. For instance, you can leverage the amount of young followers on a certain social media network to target messaging specifically to that demographic.

Metrics for email marketing

You can use data to assess the performance of your email marketing campaigns. Open and bounce rate information are widely available on email platforms. The quantity of clicks on every link is also shown. This information can be used to determine how a business stacks up against the industry standard for email marketing. You may compare campaigns internally as soon as you start measuring this data systematically. You might send an email with a 27% open rate, for instance. In the event that the internal average is 23% and the industry average is 19%, you can assess the campaign's effectiveness using your own data.

Digital marketers can enhance their ability to identify objectives and market a company's services to specific consumers by employing data analysis, which is the act of gathering and evaluating data to obtain insights. Metrics pertaining to social media, content on websites and blogs, email marketing, online adverts, and mobile downloads are

examples of data in digital marketing. Effective utilization of this data by marketers allows them to obtain insights into methods that increase the performance of their digital initiatives.

Chapter 3: Understanding the Marketing Funnel: A Complete Guide to Consumer Acquisition

A marketing funnel is a simplified representation of the path a customer takes from discovering a brand to making a purchase or using a service. The marketing funnel, often called a sales funnel, is one technique used by marketers to determine where buyers are in the purchasing process. The funnel makes it easy to provide clients with relevant content based on where they are in the buying process. Because fewer clients complete the entire process—from awareness to action—it is known as a funnel.

What Kinds of Funnels Exist?

Although the phrase "marketing funnel" refers to a broader variety of use cases, there are many different kinds of funnels:

1. Lead Funnels with Magnets:

Lead magnets are categorized as funnel marketing strategies because their purpose is to generate leads and draw others into their network. Afterwards, one may sell those leads products or services.

2. Webinar Routes:

A webinar funnel is similar to a traditional sales funnel because it serves as a lead magnet and a channel for lead conversion. The first step is to get more people to visit the landing page for your webinar. In order to turn visitors into leads at that point, information must be obtained from them.

3. Emails funnel:

The process a prospective client goes through after hearing a sales message is called an email funnel. This is typically produced by entrepreneurs to promote a goods or service through persuasive marketing techniques and educational material.

4. Social Media Marketing Funnels:

The social media marketing funnel is an effective tool that illustrates the client journey and helps you produce more leads for your business. The phrase "social media marketing funnel" describes social media-integrated marketing funnels.

5. Video Sales Funnels:

Similar to a traditional sales funnel, a video sales funnel includes engaging and memorable video content. Its objective is to draw in prospective clients, hold their attention, and eventually persuade them to become paying customers, just

like a standard sales funnel. Moreover, closing the deal is no longer the only objective.C

crucial Metrics And Analytics For Marketing Funnels

Important criteria and data in marketing tubes are essential for evaluating the success of your marketing endeavor, identifying areas that need improvement, and optimizing conversion rates. These crucial KPIs and statistics should be considered at every level of the marketing channel.

1. Business Volume

In the Stage of Mindfulness, find out the total number of visitors to your website or wharf runners. This may be referrals from social media, commercial support from hunters, and other sources. Views per page tally the number of runners that callers view; this might be a sign of how engaged they are with your content.

The click-through rate, or CTR, is the percentage of unique visitors that clicked on your announcement or content in relation to the total number of views. briolo Calculate The brio rate is the percentage of visitors to your website that hang up after seeing only one runner. It's possible that a high brio rate indicates little trade.

2. Interest Stage

Engagement Metrics Analyze information such as dwell time, runner scroll depth, and the quantity of content relations (likes, shares, and remark). These standards aid in determining how interested and involved readers are with your material.

To find the superior generation rate: calculate the volume of leads (also known as dispatch sign-ups) created in relation to the total number of visitors. This indicates that your efforts to generate leads were effective.

Use of Content Keep an eye on the places or pleasant items that are most popular to determine what your followers are interested in.

3. Level of Deliberation Rate of Conversion Calculate the percentage of leads that finish a requested effort (such downloading an eBook or cataloging a rally) in relation to all leads. This is a critical metric for evaluating the efficacy of your lead nurturing campaigns.

CTR, or click-through rate Pay attention to CTR to gauge how well your message is reaching potential customers, especially when targeting mass market titans.

Interaction with Dispatch Evaluate the open, click-through, and unsubscribe rates of your dispatch marketing campaigns to see how successful they are.

4. Conversion Rate by Stage of Conversion

This measure, which indicates the percentage of callers who finish a requested effort (such completing a purchase or obtaining a citation), is still significant at this point. Utilizing the Average Order Value (AOV) method, find the average amount of money that customers spend on a single transaction. An improved AOV might boost revenue. Rate of Shopping Basket Abandonment Find out what percentage of visitors fill their handbasket with merchandise but choose not to complete the transaction. Reducing wain abandonment is necessary to optimize conversion rates. Promotional Funnel Drop-Offs Analyze the points in the offers channel when customers quit or cease making purchases. This makes it easier to find backups of the conversion process.

5. Advocacy and Retention Stage: Customer Retention Rate: Calculate the proportion of consumers who stick with your business over time. A company's ability to retain employees over the long run depends on this.

6. Net Promoter Score (NPS): Determine customer satisfaction and loyalty by calculating NPS, which indicates the likelihood that consumers will tell others about your company.

Determine the overall value a customer brings to your company throughout their whole relationship with you by using the client lifetime value (CLV) calculation. Gaining more CLV is often more economical than acquiring new clients.

Why Are Marketing Funnels Beneficial?

Learning about the marketing channel is beneficial. You can implement a successful marketing strategy and prioritize tasks by setting up marketing tubes.There are several benefits of using marketing funnels:

1. Enhanced revenue: Through the use of a marketing funnel, companies may lead prospective clients through the many phases of the purchasing process, from awareness to acquisition. Sales and conversion rates are increased by using this methodical strategy.

2. Targeted marketing: By using marketing funnels, companies may modify their strategies and messaging to appeal to certain funnel phases. This raises the possibility of conversions by ensuring that the appropriate message reaches the correct audience at the right moment.

3. Lead generation: By gathering prospective clients' contact details, marketing funnels assist in the production of leads. By doing this, businesses may increase the likelihood of future purchases by nurturing these leads over time and fostering connections.

4. Customer insights: Businesses may watch customer activity and get useful information about their preferences, interests, and purchasing patterns by using marketing funnels. Subsequently, marketing tactics may be improved and client interactions can be made more tailored using this knowledge.

5. Scalability: Businesses may readily modify their marketing funnel tactics in accordance with their objectives, available resources, and intended audience. Because of its adaptability, marketing initiatives may change and develop with the company.

6. Return on investment (ROI): With marketing funnels, companies can monitor how well their campaigns are doing at every turn of the funnel. Businesses may maximize their return on investment by refining their marketing strategies via the analysis of critical indicators like conversion rates and cost per acquisition.

7. Clearly defined structure: To help clients through the purchasing process, marketing funnels provide a clearly defined framework. From first awareness until completing a purchase, they assist firms in comprehending the many phases and interactions that consumers go through.

8. Higher conversion rates: Organizations may boost their marketing plans and methods by outlining the customer journey and comprehending the demands of the target audience at every step. Funnels provide organizations the ability to see any gaps or obstacles that might prevent conversion and fix them.

9. Ongoing enhancement: Funnels provide companies the ability to track and improve their marketing initiatives continuously.

What distinguishes a marketing funnel from a sales funnel?

Some people combine the terms "marketing funnel" and "sales funnel" into one and refer to it as the marketing sales funnel. Actually, these two are parts of a bigger picture. The marketing and sales divisions of businesses or organizations work toward certain goals that are backed by separate channels. While marketing is in charge of creating and sustaining a brand, increasing awareness, and providing quality leads for sales, sales is focused on increasing the quantity of goods or services sold, both initially and over time. When team members collaborate to teach one another, there's a chance that the customer experience and synchronization will improve.

How to use a full-funnel strategy in your advertising:

The marketing funnel is an effective mechanism for attracting audiences. Customer journeys and conversion funnels are two distinct concepts, however. In today's industry, customers seldom go directly from awareness to consideration to purchase. It seems that customers may enter the funnel at any moment or bypass any phases completely. That is to say, although the funnel offers a helpful framework for ensuring that you're engaging customers along several routes to purchase, few client journeys will precisely match it.

Although it can be impossible to predict the actions that buyers would take prior to buying your products, a full-funnel marketing plan takes into account every avenue via which potential clients might interact with your company. This will help you find your customers wherever they may be and find opportunities for connection.

How to Create a Digital Marketing Funnel :

A whole series of marketing strategies has to be carefully thought up and implemented in order to guide potential customers from the first mindfulness stage to the final conversion. A channel for digital marketing is what this is called. This is a thorough how-to for setting up a digital marketing channel.

1. Determine Who You Want to Request It's simple to identify the perfect visitors' personalities. Share their inclinations, goals, areas of discomfort, and demographics. This information will direct your content and targeting approach.

2. Select the Phases of Your Tube The traditional stages of digital marketing funnels include awareness, interest, consideration, conversion, retention/advocacy, and then some more. Establish which specific stages are appropriate for your business, products, and services.

3. promote awareness To attract new customers, make use of a range of digital channels, such as social media, search engines, advertising, content marketing, and dispatch marketing. Create engaging and informative content, such as blog posts, videos, infographics, and social media bulletins, that speaks to the issues and interests of your audience.

4. Arouse interest Provide insightful content to your audience to educate and stimulate their interest. This hierarchy may apply to forums, ebooks, case studies, and newsletters. Request that callers join your dispatch list or follow you on social media to keep them engaged.

5. Promote Thoughtfulness Continue providing educational content that emphasizes the features and benefits of your product or service. Announcements for retargeting may help you remain in front of potential customers who are intrigued but not yet converted.

6. Encourage Conversion Create compelling calls to action (CTAs) that persuade visitors to your website to do the necessary action, such as requesting a rally, purchasing a product, or signing up for a free trial.

7. Interaction After Conversion Continue communicating with customers via social media, dispatch marketing, and tailored recommendations to keep them informed and engaged. Encourage referrals, witnesses, and business recreation to increase the value of ongoing customers.

8. Examine and refine Keep track of and estimate critical data at every point along the channel, such as revenue, open rates, conversion rates, and profit margin. Use analytics tools to identify areas for improvement, backup plans, and successful strategies. A/B test eye-catching channel elements including content, subtitles, and calls to action to help resolve problems.

9. Streamline and Expand Utilize marketing automation tools to speed up the nurturing process by providing drug users with tailored offers and information based on their level of exertion. Consider expanding your following as you improve your channel by using other marketing channels and techniques to increase the number of trials you run.

10. Provide Excellent Customer Service Providing outstanding customer service and assistance may have a tremendous impact on visitor retention and advocacy. Make sure customers like doing business with your organization.

Chapter 4: Managing the Customer Journey: From Knowledge to Persuasion

Businesses need to have a thorough grasp of their consumers and the decision-making processes they use when making purchases in today's fiercely competitive market. Increasing the awareness of a product or service is no longer sufficient; instead, enterprises must lead their customers on a journey that begins with awareness and concludes with advocacy. This journey, also referred to as the customer journey, is an essential part of any successful marketing strategy. The different phases of the customer journey will be covered in this piece, along with strategies for assisting customers in transitioning from awareness to advocacy.

Phases of the client journey:

The five phases of the customer journey are awareness, consideration, conversion, retention, and advocacy. Every stage signifies a crucial juncture in the consumer's decision-making process. Let's examine each level in further depth:

1. Awareness: During this first phase, customers learn about a business's offerings. Numerous channels, including social media, advertising, and word-of-mouth, might cause this. To stand out from the competition and draw in new clients, businesses must create powerful and memorable brand experiences.

2. Consideration: After learning about a business, customers go on to the consideration phase, during which they compare the offerings of the organization to alternatives. This is the time for firms to highlight the value they provide and showcase their USP. Using customer testimonials, providing product

demonstrations, and dispensing instructional materials are all successful strategies at this level.

3. Conversion: During this phase, customers decide whether or not to buy a product or service. Now is the crucial time for businesses to make it as simple as possible for clients to finish the transaction. Providing exceptional customer service, optimizing the purchasing process, and running specials or discounts are essential to turning leads into paying customers.

4. Retention: Fostering and establishing enduring relationships with clients is the goal of this stage. Generally speaking, keeping current customers is simpler and more economical than trying to win over new ones. To keep customers interested and pleased, businesses should concentrate on retention by offering exceptional post-purchase experiences, ongoing customer support, and incentive programs.

5. Advocacy: Advocacy is the last phase of the customer experience. At this stage, customers turn into devoted brand ambassadors who voluntarily tell others about the business. Exceeding customer expectations and delivering exceptional goods and services leads to advocacy. Companies may create advocacy via actively gathering input from customers, rewarding devoted patrons, and using social proof to highlight favorable experiences.

Methods for leading clients through the procedure:

To effectively move consumers from awareness to advocacy, businesses should use the following strategies:

1. Adopt a customer-centric mindset: Companies should always put the needs and desires of their clients first. Every touchpoint—including marketing campaigns and post-purchase support—should use the same strategy.

2. Employ data-driven marketing: Use analytics and data to understand your consumers' behaviors, preferences, and problem areas. By analyzing customer data, organizations may provide relevant information at every stage of the customer journey and customize their marketing efforts.

3. Provide interesting material: Give readers interesting, educational stuff that enhances their experience. These might be movies, blogs, postings on social media, or even live events. To position the brand as an authority in the industry, content should address the demands of the audience and alleviate any discomforts they may be experiencing.

4. Make the most of customisation by adjusting communications and products to your customers' likes and interests. A more relevant and customized experience might result from customization, which would raise conversion and advocacy rates.

5. Prioritize client retention: Implement plans to draw in new business and hold onto existing clientele. This may be offering value-added services, developing loyalty programs, or offering top-notch customer support. By prioritizing retention, businesses may boost client lifetime value and promote favorable word-of-mouth recommendations.

6. Encourage customer input: Throughout the process, actively look for customer feedback at several points of contact. Make use of these comments to improve products, services, and customer relations. Customers value companies that are more attentive to their demands and demonstrate the effectiveness of content marketing.

Chapter 5: Content marketing

Content marketing is a strategic marketing approach that aims to attract and retain a target audience via the creation and distribution of well-written, current, and engaging content. The goals of content marketing are to create material that builds brand loyalty, generates leads, provides relevant information or entertainment to potential customers, and ultimately encourages profitable customer action.

Content may include things like eBooks, infographics, podcasts, videos, blogs, social media posts, whiteapers, and more. It's critical to discreetly promote the company and its goods and services while offering high-quality content that meets the demands and interests of the intended audience. Content marketing has transformed the way companies engage with their target market and promote growth. It is now a powerful tool that brands can utilize to engage, educate, and entertain their customers while creating long-lasting relationships.

This marketing strategy has shown to be quite effective in helping businesses differentiate themselves from the competition and draw in potential clients in an authentic and unobtrusive manner. One of the key advantages of content marketing is its capacity to provide clients value that goes beyond traditional advertising strategies. Companies may establish themselves as thought leaders by creating engaging, informative, and unique content for their audience. This helps the company become recognized as an authority in its field and builds credibility and trust. Consumers who trust a firm that regularly produces useful information are more likely to become loyal supporters of that business.

Furthermore, content marketing helps companies to target certain audiences and customize their messaging for maximum impact. By producing content that precisely addresses the needs and interests of their target audience, businesses may effectively engage customers and enhance conversion rates. Businesses may increase advocacy and brand loyalty by fostering closer ties with their consumers via the use of a tailored strategy.

In addition to boosting visibility, content marketing promotes social sharing. When businesses produce interesting and valuable content, customers are motivated to share it with their networks, expanding the brand's message's audience. This organic sharing expands the brand's reach and might draw in new business and referral visitors. Another significant advantage of content marketing is its lower cost when compared to traditional forms of advertising. By producing and disseminating content online, businesses may reach a wider audience for a fraction of the cost of traditional advertising. This low-cost method of contacting a big number of potential customers is particularly beneficial for startups and small enterprises with tight marketing resources.

Content Marketing's Benefits for Online Presence

1.Boosts Website Visibility in Search Engines: Google and other search engines favor websites with original, regularly updated content. If you regularly produce excellent content, your website's search engine optimization (SEO) may be enhanced and your chances of appearing higher in search results may increase. This will facilitate finding you for potential clients.

2.Establishes Authority and Trust: Well-written material emphasizes your background and provides proof of your industry knowledge. If your target market perceives you as an authority in your field, there's a greater chance they'll seek for your products or services and trust your brand.

3.Encourages Social Media Interaction: Viral and intriguing content is a certain way to win over followers on social media. When people share your content with their network, it will greatly boost your online visibility since they are more likely to find it instructive or interesting. As a result, viral marketing might help your company become even more well-known.

4.Boosts Organic Traffic: Your unique content will be discovered by readers who are really interested in your subject via organic sources. Organic traffic has a higher conversion rate to leads or customers since the visitors are already interested in what you have to offer.

5.Enhances Awareness of Brands: Your brand remains at the forefront of your audience's thoughts when it produces strong and consistent content. As customers see your brand more often, their familiarity with it grows, enhancing trust and brand awareness.

6.Promotes Backlinks: Individuals who find your work valuable may include links to it on their blogs or websites. These backlinks not only help your website gain more authority, but they also draw in new clients.

What Does a Content Marketing Strategy Entail?

Your overall approach for producing and sharing content to expand your audience and meet various business goals is called your content marketing strategy. A few examples of content marketing are as follows:

1. Blog postings: In order to provide their target audience useful information and insights, many businesses publish blog articles. A fitness brand may, for instance, provide articles on the advantages of exercise, healthy food, and training advice.

2. material on social media: Brands publish interesting and educational material on Facebook, Twitter, and Instagram. This may contain brief industry-related advice, photos, infographics, and videos. In the end, increasing brand recognition and loyalty is the goal of drawing in and interacting with followers.

3. Videos: Businesses make videos to show off their goods or services, instruct or amuse viewers. An IT corporation may, for instance, provide instructional movies that walk viewers through the operation of its software or hardware.

4. E-books and white papers: These extended works of writing provide comprehensive information on certain subjects. Enterprises often produce e-books or white papers that consumers may get by supplying their contact details. This aids companies in generating leads and establishing their authority in the field.

5. Podcasts: As a kind of content marketing, a lot of firms are increasingly embracing podcasts. They may contact their target audience when they are resting, working out, or just driving by offering insightful and captivating audio material.

6. Infographics and other visual material: This kind of content may communicate complicated information in an easier-to-understand manner and is very shareable. One technique to convey facts and statistics in an aesthetically pleasing way is via infographics.

7. Online courses and webinars: To instruct their audience on certain subjects, brands might develop online courses or arrange webinars. By doing this, they establish credibility with prospective clients and show off their knowledge. These

are just a few of the ways businesses may utilize content marketing to reach, interact, and establish a connection with their target market. Providing high-quality, relevant, and meaningful material that aligns with the needs and interests of the audience is crucial.

What is a content plan?

An organized overview or strategy that describes the many kinds of content that will be produced and released over a certain time frame is called a content plan. It is a road plan that helps marketers, corporations, and content producers produce and disseminate high-quality, focused information that supports their aims and objectives. A content plan consists of the following elements:

1. Goals and Objectives: Clearly stated goals and objectives that the content strategy seeks to accomplish. These might include raising brand exposure, boosting website traffic, producing leads, or enhancing client interaction.

2. Target Audience: A thorough understanding of the needs, interests, problems, and demographics of the target audience. In order to make the content appealing to the intended audience, this helps change it.

3. Content Types and Formats: A range of content forms, including case studies, blog articles, podcasts, videos, infographics, webinars, and social media postings, will be generated. The objectives of the content strategy and the tastes of the target audience influence the choice of content formats.

4. Content Creation and Publishing Schedule: A comprehensive timetable indicating the dates and locations for the creation, publication, and distribution of

every piece of content. This guarantees the regular and prompt supply of material and specifies the platforms, channels, and dates on which it will be disseminated.

5. Keyword Research and SEO Strategy: To increase the visibility and discoverability of content in search engine results, relevant keywords should be found and integrated with SEO tactics.

6. material Distribution and Promotion: Ways to get the word out about the material. This might be using email marketing campaigns, distributing information on social media, working with influencers or business partners, or spending money on sponsored advertising.

7. Performance Measurement and Evaluation: Instruments and measurements to monitor each piece of content's efficacy and performance. In order to maximize subsequent content efforts, this aids in evaluating the content plan's effectiveness and making data-driven choices.

Why Develop a Content Marketing Strategy?

1. Understanding Your Target Audience: Creating a content marketing plan enables you to obtain a deep understanding of your target audience and create material that speaks to their interests and requirements.

2. Brand Awareness: Reliable and insightful content increases brand awareness, which helps your audience identify and recall your company.

3. Search Engine Optimization: Since search engines favor new, relevant, and high-quality material, a well-designed content plan may raise your website's ranks.

4.Lead Generation: By drawing in and interacting with prospective clients, strategic content may work as a formidable lead generation

tool by collecting contact details or directing visitors through the sales funnel.

5. Thought Leadership: By establishing your brand as an authoritative and educational resource in your sector, you may win over customers' confidence and credibility.

6. Competitive Edge: A strong content strategy sets you out from rivals by highlighting your USPs and setting your company apart from the competition.

7. Customer Education: You may use content to answer frequently asked questions and provide answers to concerns about your goods and services. This can help your audience make better judgments about what to buy.

8.Social Media Presence: Viral material is more likely to become viral when it is shareable and interesting content builds community on social media.

9. Increased client loyalty may be attained by consistently producing high-quality content that engages your audience and fortifies the bond between your business and its patrons.

10. Flexibility to Trends: You may effectively adjust your brand to shifting consumer interests and industry trends by using a flexible content marketing approach.

11.Cost-Effectiveness: When weighed against conventional advertising, content marketing may be more affordable, particularly in light of its long-term advantages and potential for organic reach.

12. Measurement and Analytics: Using a content strategy, you can monitor and assess the effectiveness of your material to learn what works and how to maximize your efforts for greater outcomes.

13. Multi-Channel Reach: A well planned approach makes sure your material is shared on several platforms, reaching a wider audience and accommodating a range of tastes.

14. Optimization of Conversions: By offering relevant information at the appropriate moment, material tailored for various phases of the buyer's journey may maximize conversions.

15. Flexible to Different forms: A content marketing plan enables you to test out various content forms, like podcasts, infographics, videos, blog posts, and more, to accommodate a range of audience tastes.

16.Enhanced online visibility: The more regularly you post, the more potential customers you may attract. Provide customers with informative, useful information that addresses their areas of concern.

17.Increased leads: By drawing in visitors, a successful content marketing strategy may boost leads.

Increased power If you keep producing insightful material, people in your industry will eventually see you as an expert.

18.Enhanced communication with clients: Loyal customers often bring in repeat business. Speak with those who comment on your posts or respond to you.

19.More funding: If you can show that your marketing is productive, it should be easier to ask for a bigger marketing budget in the future.

Chapter 6: Techniques for Telling Stories in Content Marketing

"Storytelling" in content marketing refers to using storytelling strategies to engage your target audience and promote your business. Using a story in your marketing materials may help you create a deeper emotional connection with readers in addition to grabbing their attention.

You may improve your brand's relatability, memorability, and gripping power by employing tales to humanize it. Whatever sort of content you're creating—blog articles, videos, social media campaigns, or anything else—narrative is a potent weapon that might help you stand out in a competitive digital marketplace and achieve your marketing goals.

The value of storytelling in content marketing:

What makes storytelling so crucial in content marketing is its capacity to establish a connection with your target audience and effectively communicate your company's message. In today's fast-paced, digital world, people are continuously exposed to an excessive amount of information. To stand out from the crowd and capture their interest, you need to provide content that is both distinctive and relevant to them. That's when the story starts to work.

By using storytelling, you may arouse emotions in your audience, bring your brand to life, and develop stronger relationships with them. Effective use of storytelling may help you stand out from the competition, increase interaction with your target audience, and offer your business a unique voice and personality. Using stories into your content may also increase its effectiveness, memorability, and shareability, all of which may boost consumer loyalty, brand awareness, and conversion rates. Put another way, a successful content marketing plan requires storytelling.

How to choose the best narrative for your material:

Making the right story choice for your material is critical to the success of any storytelling projects. A captivating narrative should not only captivate readers but also correspond with your brand statement and marketing goals. The following should be considered before selecting a story:

1.Who is the target market for you? What interests them, what pains them, and what preferences do they have? Which tales are the most likely to pique their interest and encourage interaction?

2.Your statement on your brand: What message do you want to convey with your material? What are your brand values, and how can you apply them to your story?

3.Your marketing goals: What action do you want your audience to do after they've read or seen your information? How might your narrative help achieve those goals?

4.Relevance: Make sure your story makes sense for your target audience as well as the present situation.

5.Emotion: A good story should evoke strong feelings in you, whether they be ones of joy, inspiration, or grief. Choose a narrative that will probably evoke the emotions you want to portray.

Once you've selected a story that resonates with your target audience, brand message, and marketing goals, you can start crafting your content around it. Remember that choosing the appropriate story to convey is not the only step in creating a compelling and effective narrative.

The significance of emotions in narrative for content marketing:

Emotions play a major role in storytelling for content marketing. When utilized effectively, narrative may evoke emotions in your target audience, deepening your connection with them and giving your content more relevance and memorable qualities. In addition to gaining attention, you can also affect behavior and motivate action by appealing to emotions.

If you stop to think about it, the stories that arouse strong emotions in us usually stay with us the longest. Whether a story is funny or scary, it is likely to be shared and remembered if it makes us feel something. Similar to this, by using emotional appeals in your content marketing, you may create a closer bond with your target audience and inspire them to share your material with others.

When it comes to emotions, there isn't a single answer that suits everyone. People will relate to different emotions, therefore it's critical to identify your target market and create a narrative that will probably evoke the emotions that support your business goals. Pick a narrative that is likely to arouse the feelings—such as inspiration, happiness, or empathy—that are significant to your company and your target audience.

The several storytelling strategies used in content marketing:

The greatest form of story to use in your content marketing will depend on your brand, your target audience, and your goals. There are many different approaches to develop a narrative. In content marketing, some of the most popular storytelling methods are:

1. Personal tales: To communicate relatable real-life experiences with their audience, content marketers often turn to personal narratives. These narratives, which seek to emotionally engage and connect with readers, may include experiences, setbacks, or triumphs.

2. Customer testimonials: Sharing testimonials from customers is a great way to tell a narrative since it establishes a product or service's legitimacy and offers social proof. To illustrate the worth and advantages of their products, content marketers use true accounts of delighted clients.

3. Case studies: Case studies are in-depth narratives that illustrate how a goods or service helped a client with a particular issue. They often provide comprehensive details on the customer's journey, obstacles encountered, and outcomes attained. Case studies demonstrate how a business produces measurable benefits for a client, which helps create authority and foster confidence.

4. narrative arcs and cliffhangers: You may keep readers interested and captivated by developing a sequence of content pieces with a gripping narrative arc or by

using cliffhangers in blog entries or social media updates. This narrative approach raises the likelihood of conversions or brand loyalty by encouraging readers to remain engaged with the company's content.

5. Brand genesis tales: Telling the tale of a brand's beginnings, difficulties encountered, and goals fosters a stronger bond with the target market. Customers may more closely associate themselves with the brand's ideals and become devoted brand supporters by learning about the brand's journey.

6. User-generated content: One effective storytelling tactic is to encourage clients to contribute their tales by means of user-generated content (UGC) programs. It gives consumers the opportunity to actively participate in the brand's story and offers social proof, which has the power to draw in and persuade potential buyers.

7. Emotional appeal: To establish a bond with the audience, storytelling techniques often make use of emotional appeal. Companies tell stories that make readers laugh, feel happy, feel empathetic, or feel nostalgic in order to connect with readers on a deeper level.

8. Keeping the audience in mind: Skilled content marketers recognize their target and build narratives that speak to their wants and desires. Brands may increase engagement and foster trust by producing content that speaks directly to the needs, problems, and goals of their target audience.

9. Visual storytelling: The narrative process may be improved by including visuals like pictures, films, or infographics. Visual components make knowledge easier to remember by drawing the viewer in, improving informational effectiveness, and evoking strong emotions.

10. Interactive storytelling: By using interactive components like polls, surveys, and quizzes, you may increase audience engagement and involvement. Interactive

storytelling is a useful tool for companies to gather important data, get insights, and improve user personalization.

11. Industry storytelling: This kind of storytelling focuses on the overall industry and how your company operates within it. Using thought-provoking articles, trade journals, and other content kinds that establish your brand as an expert in your industry are some ways to do this.

Techniques for writing compelling narratives:

Creating a compelling narrative is the key to successful storytelling in content marketing. An engaging story should enthrall your target audience, complement your brand strategy and marketing goals, and evoke strong feelings in them that strengthen your connection to them. You could find the following methods useful in crafting gripping narratives:

Remember your audience: Make sure your narrative resonates with the needs, interests, and pain points of your intended audience. If your story is more relevant to your target audience, they will be more inclined to relate to it.

Begin with a hook: What grabs readers or viewers and persuades them to keep reading or watching your story is called a hook. This may be an intriguing story, a perplexing query, or an unexpected revelation.

Build tension: A good story should include conflict and tension, whether it is a fight to achieve a goal or a dilemma that has to be resolved. You may keep your audience engaged and interested in the tale by building tension.

Use vivid images in conjunction with comprehensive language to assist your readers picture what you're talking about. Your tale will become more memorable and impactful as a result.

Don't tell, show: Give your viewers some images to go along with the information you are discussing. Increase the interest level of your story by using pictures, stories, and other components.

Create an emotional connection: An engaging narrative should evoke emotions in the audience that result in a stronger relationship. Choose a story that will most likely arouse emotions relevant to your business and target audience.

Stay basic: An engaging story should be easy to read and comprehend. Prevent your story from being too convoluted or twisted. Stay brief and focus on the primary point.

Typical narrative errors in content marketing that should be avoided:

Storytelling is an effective content marketing technique, but in order to ensure that your stories are engaging and fruitful, you must avoid common pitfalls. Remember these typical pitfalls when using story in content marketing:

1. Lack of focus: A clear and distinct storyline is necessary. If your tale is too disjointed or unfocused, it is unlikely to captivate readers and accomplish your marketing goals.

2. Inauthenticity: Your audience will be able to detect if your story looks forced or out of the ordinary. Make sure the stories you share are true to yourself and in line with your company's objectives and core values.

3. Lack of powerful emotions: Stories that don't stir up strong emotions aren't going to make an impression. Make sure your stories create a stronger emotional connection and hold the attention of your readers.

4. Disregarding your readers: The narrative ought to center on them, not on you. Make sure your tale will be relevant and engaging to the audience you are writing for.

5. Ignoring the call to action: Ensure that there is a clear call to action in your narrative content. The reader should feel compelled by your tale to take some action, whether it is signing up for your email list, making a purchase, or something else completely.

6. Overcomplicating the story: Make sure your story is clear and easy to grasp. If your tale is too intricate or convoluted, neither your audience nor your marketing goals will be engaged.

By avoiding these typical blunders, you can ensure that your content marketing story is compelling, successful, and fulfills your marketing goals. Your storytelling endeavors will be fruitful if you focus on telling stories that are relevant, meaningful, and helpful.

The following guidelines may help you weave a narrative across your whole content marketing strategy:

Although using stories in your content marketing might be beneficial, it's crucial to use them carefully and systematically throughout the whole process. You might use the following tactics to do it:

1. Commence with your brand narrative: Your brand story should be the focal point of any content marketing plan you implement, including any efforts involving storytelling. Make sure the story behind your brand makes sense and appeals to the intended audience.

2. Write a story that will appeal to your target audience after deciding who they are. Find out the hobbies and demographics of your target audience and what sorts of stories would most likely spark their interest.

3. Use narrative techniques in a range of media: Every content marketing campaign, including email campaigns, social media postings, and blog pieces, should have a backstory.

4. Make it visually appealing: Images may significantly increase the impact of your story. Consider using photos, movies, and other visual components to bring your tale to life and grab the audience's attention.

5. Evaluate your results: Exercise care while evaluating the outcomes of your storytelling projects. Keep an eye on crucial information like engagement, internet traffic, and conversions. Over time, use this knowledge to refine and improve your storytelling style.

6. Continue being consistent: Telling tales in content marketing requires consistency. Make sure the stories you provide are consistent with your company's mission, core values, and content marketing plan.

With the help of these strategies, you can effectively include storytelling into your whole content marketing campaign and create captivating content that appeals to your target audience.

Making Captivating Digital Marketing Content: Six Essential Factors to Take Into Account:

In today's competitive digital market, producing top-notch marketing material is more crucial than ever for businesses and brands hoping to expand online. To ensure that your content strategy is effective, you need to consider these six essential components:

1. An emphasis on the viewer

The first step to successful digital marketing is having a deep grasp of your target demographic. Before you begin creating any content, take some time to understand the needs, preferences, demographics, and areas of concern of your audience. Personalization is necessary to properly engage potential consumers. If you address their concerns and aspirations directly, there's a greater chance that your message will be understood and converted.

2. Clearly stated objectives and a strategy:

Before you start writing content, decide what your marketing objectives are. Are you looking to boost revenue, get leads, or build awareness of your brand? Your writing must be relevant to these goals. Create a comprehensive content plan that specifies the kind and frequency of material you will publish. A good internet presence requires the creation and distribution of information on a regular basis.

3. Improved Observation:

Finding quality content is only one aspect of the issue. Make use of SEO (Search Engine Optimization) best practices to make your content more visible in search results. Employing SEO strategies and pertinent keywords might raise the position of your content in search results.

4. Strong Proposition of Value:

Every word you write ought to convey the special value that your product or service delivers. Describe to your audience how it allays their worries or accomplishes their goals. This value proposition and the benefits of the product you're selling should be highlighted in your essay.

5. Using Pictures and Narrative to Activate:

In the very visual digital world of today, having excellent photos, videos, and graphics may greatly enhance your message. Because people remember tales more than facts and data, craft engrossing narratives that emotionally link your audience and successfully express your company's message. It might be advantageous to use tales to establish a stronger, more enduring connection with your audience.

6. Decision-Making Based on Information:

In the field of digital marketing, wingmanning is a thing of the past. It is crucial to base decisions on knowledge and experience. You may use analytics software and key performance indicators (KPIs) to evaluate the efficacy of your material. A/B testing may be used to determine the most popular material among your audience, and data analysis facilitates the process of revising your plan and content. You may be able to make decisions that result in better outcomes if you closely monitor the effectiveness of your material.

Chapter 7: Content Optimization for Search Engines

In search engine optimization (SEO), content optimization refers to writing and presenting material in a manner that search engines can comprehend and deliver to your intended audience. Making sure your site's pages are appealing to visitors and search engines alike is the essence of the procedure. Alongside SEO, good content optimization lays the groundwork for websites that perform well.

The process of improving online material for search engines and consumers alike involves increasing exposure, relevancy, and usability. This is known as content optimization. In order to increase the effectiveness and ranking of web pages, blog posts, articles, videos, and other digital material, it entails a variety of tactics.

More organic search engine traffic, user engagement, and persuasion to do desired actions—like buying something, signing up for a subscription, or sharing the material with others—are the ultimate goals of content optimization.

Understanding the target audience and their search intent is crucial for content optimization. When it comes to figuring out what terms and phrases visitors are looking for that are relevant to the content, keyword research is essential. To increase the material's exposure in search engine results, these keywords may then be thoughtfully included to the text, meta tags, headers, and URL structure.

material optimization also entails producing original, useful, and high-quality material that speaks to the target audience's requirements and interests. Using captivating headlines, making the material readable via formatting, using photos and videos, and organizing the text with pertinent headers and subheadings are all examples of this.

Technical optimization is also a crucial component of content optimization. This entails, among other things, optimizing the URL structure, internal linking, metadata, loading speed, and responsiveness to mobile devices. Technical optimization guarantees trouble-free user access and navigation as well as efficient crawling and indexing of the material by search engines.

For what reason is content optimization crucial?

SEO requires careful consideration of content optimization. Only well-optimized individual pieces of content will get high search engine ranking. The greatest opportunity for your content to rank well and get plenty of organic traffic is to optimize it.

1. Enhanced Search Engine Ranking: By making your website more visible to search engines, content optimization raises its ranks and boosts organic traffic.

2. Improved User Experience: Users have a better overall experience when they interact with material that has been optimized to present them with worthwhile information.

3. Tailored Audience Reach: Optimizing your content to target certain keywords and themes will draw in a more niche audience that is interested in what you have to offer.

4. Higher Conversions: Effectively optimized content may direct users through the conversion funnel by offering pertinent details and attention-grabbing calls to action.

5. Decreased Bounce Rates: Site visitors are more likely to stick around after finding what they're searching for, thus relevant and optimized content lowers bounce rates.

6. Mobile Compatibility: To accommodate the increasing number of mobile users, content optimization makes sure that it can be accessed and read on a range of devices, such as tablets and smartphones.

7. Faster Page Loading Times: Your website will function better overall if your content is optimized to minimize page loading times.

8. Establishing your brand as an expert in your sector with high-quality, optimized content helps you gain the audience's confidence and credibility.

9. Adjusting to Algorithm Changes: Optimised content assists your website in adjusting to the regular changes in search engine algorithms, which helps you keep or raise your ranks.

10. Competitive Edge: You attract more visitors and prospective consumers by continuously improving your content, which keeps you ahead of rivals who may not be making the same effort.

11. Efficient Use of Keywords: material optimization makes sure that pertinent keywords are strategically placed, which facilitates search engines' comprehension and ranking of your material.

12. Improved Social Media Visibility: Shared on social media, optimized content is more likely to expand your audience and bring in more visitors to your website.

13. Compliance with accessibility standards: Enhancing the accessibility of your material will make it more inclusive for visitors with impairments.

14. Data-Driven Decision Making: By examining user behavior and data, optimization enables you to make well-informed choices on how to enhance and customize your content for improved outcomes.

How to Optimize Content:

1.Practice keyword research:After figuring out what information potential clients in your target market are looking for about certain product or service possibilities, it's time to do some keyword research. You must do keyword research before creating any content to make sure that your topics relate to the search phrases that people in your target audience are currently using. If your content fulfills user expectations and receives a substantial amount of monthly searches, search engines will rank it higher, preferably at the top of the search engine results page (SERP).

If you don't do keyword research, you have a lesser chance of meeting the needs, preferences, and topic expectations of prospective clients.

2. Verify Spelling and GrammarInaccurate spelling and punctuation are the easiest things to make a website seem less trustworthy. Before publishing, verify your writing many times using a spell checker.

3. Establish Internal Connectivity

It makes sense to provide internal links to other pertinent material on your website. This increases Google's indexing speed for these sites and increases your likelihood of appearing in search results.

4. Make Use of Multimedia

A lengthy text block without any breaks is the worst thing that can happen to readers.

screenshot with embedded video for food blog content optimization

Photo credit: A Pinch of Yum

Including pictures, graphics, and videos in your material is a terrific method to keep people interested and extend their stay.

5. Remember to Use Title Tags and Meta Descriptions: Make captivating title tags and meta descriptions to draw readers in as they peruse the search results.

How Can I Tell Whether the Content on My Website Needs to be Optimized?

1. Content optimization can significantly improve your site if you are not targeting any particular keywords. Your pages will rank higher if you concentrate on a small number of target keywords.

2. Does your material show up on search engine results pages? material optimization can help your web pages if the response is negative and you are unable to locate your material on the first few pages.

3. If your material is ranked lower on page 1 or page 2, content optimization will probably provide it a swift boost to go up the SERPs.

Tools with content Optimization features:

You may optimize your content with the help of a number of tools. Below are a few well-known ones:

1. Google Analytics: This tool lets you know about user activity on your website, traffic, and how people are interacting with your content.

2. Google Search Console: Assists in tracking how well your website performs in Google Search, allows you to upload sitemaps, and helps you find and address problems that might be affecting your site's search engine rankings.

3. Yoast SEO: This WordPress plugin offers real-time advice for enhancing your on-page SEO and assists you in optimizing your content for search engines.

4. SEMrush: Provides a range of tools to help you maximize your content strategy, including competition and backlink analysis, keyword research, and more.

5.Ahrefs: Offers resources for backlink analysis, content discovery, and keyword research, assisting you in identifying your rivals and tailoring your material to their strategies.

6. Moz: Provides tools for link analysis, site audits, and keyword research to assist you enhance the search engine performance of your content.

7. Grammarly: A writing aid that proofreads your work for grammatical and spelling mistakes, enhancing its polish and professionalism.

8. BuzzSumo: Assists with content ideation and optimization by assisting you in identifying trendy topics and material within your business.

9. Hootsuite: This tool lets you plan and organize social media postings so that your material is successfully shared on many channels.

10. SEOptimer: Offers a website auditing tool that checks your website for search engine optimization problems and makes suggestions for enhancements.

11.CoSchedule Headline Analyzer: Assists in crafting attention-grabbing headlines that enhance the likelihood of clicks and interaction.

12. Google PageSpeed Insights: Evaluates how well your web pages work and offers recommendations for accelerating page loads.

13. Canva: An infographic and picture creation tool to improve your content.

14. OptinMonster: An application that helps you create opt-in forms and pop-ups to turn website visitors into leads and customers.

15. BuzzStream: Promotes your content via influencers by helping with connection building and influencer outreach.

16. Surfer SEO: This additional content assistant tool provides you with a comprehensive content strategy for the subject of your choice with only a few clicks. By offering details on the appropriate word count, better keywords to employ, the structure to adhere to, and much more, it helps you outrank your rivals. Surfer offers a comprehensive checklist to help you determine what is missing from your articles and how to add it in order to improve your position and increase organic traffic for any of your content that isn't appearing on Google's first page.

17. Frase: Users may design their content using this highly automated and user-friendly content optimization tool, which helps their content rank and convert. This tool's usage of artificial intelligence to respond to inquiries from your target audience as well as provide suggestions for content optimization is a great feature. It leverages information from all the resources on your website, including product catalogs, blog entries, and landing pages, to provide critical insights.

18. ScaleNut: Designed to streamline the whole SEO lifecycle, Scalenut is an AI-powered solution. Your web pages will perform well in search engine rankings thanks to its guidance on content development, production, optimization, and analysis, which is designed to make your SEO approach simpler. Scalenut is

unique because of its data-driven suggestions that are customized to your content requirements. Its Traffic Analyzer may point out holes in the material you already have and provide suggestions on how to make it more effective for search engines. Fix-it features enable you to automatically improve Featured Snippets, H-Tags, Meta tags, NLP key phrases, and more, increasing the effectiveness and focus of content optimization.

19. GrowthBar: The SEO tool for expanding websites is called GrowthBar. It generates content outlines with keywords, word count ranges, headlines, reference links, and even pictures that best fit your subject using OpenAI GPT-3. Because of all of this, content planning is simple. It's a single kind of SEO tool that does everything. One of its best advantages is that it displays the backlinks, organic keywords, Facebook Ads, and Google Ads of your competitors, highlighting their marketing approach.

Additionally, this solution includes a lightweight software that gives writers access to a wealth of SEO data, enabling them to rank higher and increase return on investment.

20. Break Word: When developing content strategies that are in line with search engine results, Dash word is a fantastic resource. All you need to add for your next blog article is a single click. Additionally, the tool compares your content with that of the highest-ranking companies.

It informs you how lengthy your article should be and reveals the queries your audience searches for, which makes your content more relevant. Additionally, it gives your article a content score. The likelihood of ranking highly increases with score.

How to Build an SEO-Friendly Website:

In order to compete in today's online marketplace, you must make adjustments to your website for search engine optimization (SEO). Search engine queries, such as those made on Google, start around 68% of online encounters. Because of this, having your web pages show up as the top search result has many advantages, such as improving organic traffic and the authority of your website.

1. Use Keywords Throughout Your material: SEO-friendly material is essential for raising your website's ranking on search engine results pages (SERPs).
Use relevant keywords while writing blog posts to make your website more visible to search engines. By doing keyword research, you may get them.

You might get more similar phrases in the search engine results when you type in your primary keyword. When you search for pet toys, for instance, you may also see results for dog toys and pet supplies.
2. Make use of header tags
Making effective use of header tags is another method for building an SEO-friendly website. They are HTML elements that aid in the organization and interpretation of a web page's content by search engines.

<h1> through <h6> HTML components make up header tags. As the title and heads of the text are often included in <h1> and <h2> tags, pay special attention to them. Make a list of your keywords and use them in these tags appropriately.

After all <h1> elements have been optimized, try to add pertinent SEO keywords to other headers as well. To raise your SEO ranks, use this technique regularly each time you create material.

Because of this, search engine crawlers will be able to appropriately index your website for relevant information and will be aware that this page has content associated with those phrases. By doing this, you may target the proper audience and raise your page ranking in the SERPs.

3. Maintain a Clear URL Architecture

Building an SEO-friendly website requires a well-organized URL structure. An SEO-friendly URL needs to be clear, easy to read, and relevant to the content of the website.

SEO-friendly URLs make it easier for search engines to grasp what information is on each page since they are used by search engines to crawl and index websites. To do this, include the desired term into the URL.

An SEO-friendly website design page's URL, for instance, may be www.examplewebsite.com/seo-web-design.

Steer clear of lengthy query strings that include numbers, such as /top-23-seo-web-design-practises-in-2023-for-top-professionals, since this might hinder their readability and SEO value.

SEO-friendly URLs help search engines scan your website more quickly and precisely, which raises its ranking in relevant search results.

4. Use Keyword-Dense Anchor Text in Your Connections

When a user clicks on an anchor text, they are sent to a different page or area of the website. By using SEO-friendly anchor texts, material may be better understood by search engines, which raises its ranking.

You should concentrate on using keywords that are relevant to your website when crafting an SEO-friendly anchor text.

Find terms or expressions that best convey the meaning of the text and use them. Use anchor text like "Learn SEO tips" or "SEO strategies" when connecting to a website that provides SEO advice, for instance.

Keep in mind that SEO-friendly anchor texts should convey the topic of the material to search engines and be relevant to the linked page. Also, it's critical to refrain from cluttering your anchor text with keywords as this might lower the website's SEO rating.

5. Check to See If the Website Is Mobile-Friendly.

Not only does content optimization play a significant role in creating an SEO-friendly website, but mobile website development is also a crucial component.

Indeed, during the second quarter of 2022, mobile users accounted for approximately 59% of all website traffic worldwide. Because of this, mobile friendliness is a major consideration for Google and other search engines when ranking results for a given website.

This means that on mobile devices, your website needs to load swiftly. It is important to make sure the design of your website is responsive, meaning it can fit various screen sizes.

Thankfully, there is usually a mobile version included with most pre-made themes for WordPress or other website languages.

Remember to use resources such as Google's Mobile-Friendly Test to verify if your website satisfies the latest requirements.

6. Refine Pictures

Improving the visibility of your website in search engines is possible with image optimization for SEO. Make sure your photos are optimized for search engines by following these procedures, which will improve your SEO results.

Be careful you provide a suitable file name to every photograph. Keywords associated with the image's content need to be included. Improved presence on the

SERPs may result from search engines being able to better understand the image's content.

Prior to uploading your photos to your website, make sure they are smaller. Greater file sizes may cause your website to load more slowly, which might harm its SEO outcome.

To shrink your photos without sacrificing quality, think about compressing them. Image optimization for websites may be achieved by WordPress users using programs such as Smush and Image Optimizer.

Don't forget to provide alternate text for every picture as well. When an image cannot be loaded correctly, alt text—a short piece of HTML code that represents the picture's content—will show.

Incorporating this data enhances your SEO performance by assisting search engines in understanding the context of photos.

In conclusion, contemplate including brief descriptions underneath your pictures. Enhancing user experience may also result from adding more context to the visuals.

7. Verify the Speed at Which Your Websites Open

Websites with fast loading times and great user experiences are given priority by search engines. Customer satisfaction will drop, search engine crawling will be more difficult, and your SEO efforts will be negatively impacted by a sluggish website. Thankfully, optimizing your website may be accomplished in a number of ways, such as:

1.Streamline HTTP queries to speed up server response times.

2. Reduce the size without sacrificing quality of photographs and other media assets by compressing them.

3. Use browser caching to prevent the need for repetitive downloads by storing frequently requested data locally in each user's browser.

4. Use a content distribution network (CDN) to spread the weight of hosting movies, pictures, and other static material among many servers located all over the globe.

5. Invest in more bandwidth-rich web hosting.

Think about using resources like Google's PageSpeed tips to see if your website satisfies the requirements and to get a variety of tips about how to accelerate its loading time.

8. Use Social Media to Promote Your Content One of the greatest methods to make a website that is optimized for search engines is to promote it on social media platforms. With more people able to access your material, search engines will crawl and rank your website higher due to the increased number of backlinks.

It takes a combination of abilities and expertise to build your brand on social media. Additionally, in order to concentrate your efforts on the appropriate channels, you must know which social media networks, according to your specialty, might generate meaningful traffic.When it comes to some areas like fashion and cuisine, Pinterest and Instagram, for instance, may generate the fewest external website visits overall, but they might be useful.

And lastly, remember to include calls to action (CTAs) and referral links in your articles and profile. More people will visit your website if you create eye-catching CTAs with obvious messaging.

9. Employ Google Tools

Examining a website's primary metrics is a crucial part of building an SEO-friendly website. Several analytics solutions, such as Google Analytics and Search Console, are available to website owners to get this data.

With so many of these tools being free, you shouldn't worry if you have a tight budget.

The Google Search Console provides website owners with an overview of their sites' performance in Google search results.

Knowing which keywords users use to locate your material and how Google sees it may be gained from the data. In accordance with Google's recommendations, it provides you with a summary of the amount of organic traffic you have received and offers you suggestions for enhancing your website's exposure.

Along with helping you find several problems that might lower your search engine results, this tool also offers thorough reports on any content faults discovered on your website. Duplicate material, improper meta tags, and broken links are examples of these issues.Though unrelated to SEO, Google Analytics may also be helpful in providing you with a range of data to assist you enhance the overall performance of your website. The report on the page with the greatest bounce rate, for instance, is available to you.

This makes it feasible for you to accurately determine the issue's potential source and implement the required solutions.

10. Make the Site Code Clean and Organized

The many lines of code that operate different functionalities make up your website. With the expansion of your website, these code segments may become disorganized and interfere with one another. Cleaning them up as needed is advised to avoid this.

Additionally, by following this procedure, your website may load more quickly and be more easily indexed by search engines. Your website's SEO success is greatly influenced by these two essential components.

Programming languages used to create websites might vary widely. Among these, HTML, CSS, and JavaScript are the most popular. They are arranged differently in each of these languages.

Luckily, there are programs like JS Beautifier, HTML Cleaner, and Dirty Markup that may assist you in the process.

11. Include internal links

Linking other pages or posts on your website using hyperlinks embedded inside your text is known as internal linking. This builds a network of connected material and aids search engines in understanding the organization and significance of individual pages.

It is possible to include an internal link using buttons, graphics, or text.

To make sure your internal links work, take into account how relevant each page and post is that you want to connect. To facilitate the indexing process, place links on anchor texts that correspond with the destination sites' relevant context.

Another way to lower bounce rates is by strategic internal connecting. Users can more easily traverse the website and locate the appropriate material. You can also entice readers to investigate and interact with your website further by including links to similar external information in your blog entries.

Just watch out not to go overboard. A cluttered appearance and a poor user experience might result from using an excessive number of internal links in your content. To increase the SEO friendliness of your website and optimize your internal linking, use tools such as Yoast SEO, Link Whisper, and Internal Link Juicer.

12. Make the most of the Meta descriptions and title tags

HTML components that put a page's content in context include title tags and meta descriptions. While a meta description provides brief summaries of the content readers might anticipate on the page, a title tag displays on search engine results pages as clickable headlines.

When creating a title tag, make sure the focus keyword for the content is included. In order to make your material show up in the appropriate search result, it usually should correspond with the search intent of the target audience.

Don't exceed 50–60 characters for your title tag. By doing this, companies can be certain that they show up correctly in search results and increase their likelihood of drawing in readers.

However, a meta description offers you more room to acquaint prospective readers with the information. The length of a meta description is not restricted, however keep in mind that Google SERPs only display 155–160 characters.

Every meta description you write should be distinct and provide pertinent details for your intended audience. To make it more search engine friendly, you may also include long-tail keywords.

Make an effort to craft a captivating meta description that highlights the value your material offers to the prospective reader.

13. Use Pictures and Videos to Make the Content Better

Videos and other visual components may enhance and improve the readability of your material. Graphs and charts are examples of visual aids that help you convey information and convey ideas more successfully.

Videos and photos may improve your content's SEO friendliness in addition to these other advantages. By enabling your material to show up in the picture and video tab of Google search results, media files increase the likelihood that users will click on it.

Additionally, a rich snippet of your material may come up, providing extra details and increasing its likelihood of ranking well in search results.

To keep your website loading quickly, don't forget to include optimized photos and videos. Compressing the size of photos and videos and providing relevant alt text are essential components of optimization.

To simplify the process, WordPress users may also utilize plugins like Imagify and Optimole.

14. Continually Update Your Content

A fantastic SEO tactic is to constantly create fresh content. But sometimes, it might be challenging to think of original content ideas. You may enhance the SEO of your website by updating outdated material in certain situations.

Altering between producing new material and upgrading older ones will draw in new users and keep them coming back to the website. To keep your target audience engaged, make sure the material you provide speaks to the issues of the day.

Remember that offering your visitors helpful content is just as important as putting effective SEO methods into practice. Be sure the material you produce for your website adds value to your readers and enhances the reputation of your business.

Chapter 8: Optimization on- and off-page Improving the Effect on Search Outcomes:

Page optimization, also known as on-page SEO, is the term used to describe all the activities that may be taken directly on the website to improve its position in search results. Examples of this include content optimization and the improvement of title and meta tags. The practice of improving your website's pages for both search engines and visitors is known as page SEO, or search engine optimization. The process of making website content user friendly is often called "on-page SEO" or "on-site SEO." Typical on-page SEO strategies include optimized URLs, internal links, title tags, and content.

These days, page optimization includes intelligent keyword targeting, which involves referencing keywords in significant sections while maintaining a favorable user experience. This shows that your material flows well and that the reader discovers what they're really looking for. On-page SEO is the practice of optimizing individual web pages to rank higher and get more relevant visits from search engines. The word "page" refers to both the text and the HTML source code of a page that may be optimized, while off-page SEO refers to links and other external signals.

The goal of on-page optimizations, which you may do to improve your website's position or visibility in search results on Google, Bing, and other search engines, is to make your website more useful and helpful to visitors. You should focus on the more intricate aspects of page optimization after you have mastered the principles of on-page SEO.

You may improve each of these components and make your website more difficult to access while also increasing its search engine ranking. We advise using On Page SEO Checker to handle prospective page optimization ideas for your website, even though there are several on-page SEO suggested practices to consider while creating any content. Optimizing user experience is a crucial part of your on-page SEO strategy when it comes to brain ranking.

Every part of the website is suitably optimized for increased exposure and ranks in SERPs (Search Engine Results Pages) because of on-page SEO. It also improves organic traffic from visitor searches since it increases the likelihood that visitors will discover what they're searching for on your website.

Furthermore, you may raise the likelihood of obtaining higher click-through rates by using on-page SEO tactics, such as including pertinent keywords throughout the text. This will help your business generate more leads and sales.

What does off-page optimization entail?

The technique of increasing a website's visibility, authority, and ranking in search engines by using techniques not found on the website itself is known as off-page SEO. This covers content marketing, social media marketing, link-building, and other strategies to increase a business's or website's online visibility.

1. Link building: Link building is the process of obtaining backlinks to your website from other websites in an effort to improve search engine results. The technique of making connections with prominent figures in the field and using

those connections to drive more traffic to your website or company is known as social media marketing.

2. Social media marketing: Using different social media platforms to interact with consumers and promote website content in order to raise brand awareness and drive traffic.

3. Social bookmarking: Adding links to websites on social bookmarking platforms such as Digg, Reddit, and Stumble Upon may assist drive targeted traffic and increase website exposure.

4. Online reputation management: Keeping an eye on and overseeing a company's or website's online reputation by proactive customer service, answering reviews, and resolving any unfavorable remarks or criticism.

5. material marketing: Producing excellent, shareable material that can raise brand awareness, get connections from other websites, and create social media shares.

6. Influencer outreach: Working together with experts in the field and influencers to market your website, goods, or services and reach a larger audience.

7. Guest blogging: Composing and posting blog entries or articles on other respectable websites or blogs in order to develop backlinks, raise brand recognition, and improve website traffic.

8. Forum engagement: Taking part in relevant online communities and forums by actively contributing to conversations, responding to queries, and offering insightful commentary along with a backlink to your website.

9. Local SEO strategies include building Google My Business listings, submitting your website to local directories, and obtaining favorable evaluations from clients in order to optimize it for local search.

A thorough SEO plan must include off-page optimization as it raises a website's search engine ranks by assisting search engines in determining the popularity, relevancy, and authority of a certain website.

The Advantages of Off-Page and On-Page SEO

The following are the advantages of both on-page and off-page SEO:

Benefits of on-page SEO:

1. Higher ranking: You may raise the likelihood that search engines will identify your website as relevant and list it higher in search results by optimizing the content of your website, including keywords, meta tags, and page titles.

2. Greater website visibility: By ensuring sure your website is user- and search engine-friendly, on-page SEO increases its exposure in search engine results pages (SERPs).

3. Improved user experience: By making your website easier to use, quicker to load, and more navigable, on-page SEO aims to improve user experience. This improves the performance of the website as a whole by increasing user engagement and lowering bounce rates.

4. Enhanced relevancy: On-page SEO helps search engines comprehend the context and relevance of your website to certain search queries by optimizing your content with relevant keywords, tags, and headers.

Benefits of off-page SEO:

1. Enhanced website authority: The goal of off-page SEO is to increase your website's credibility and authority by acquiring backlinks from reliable websites.

Search engines see these backlinks as votes of confidence, which raises the authority and search engine rating of your website.

2. Increased online presence: You may make your company more visible online by using off-page SEO strategies like influencer collaborations, content promotion, and social media marketing. Your website may see an increase in visitors, visibility, and viewership as a consequence of this.

3. Greater brand exposure: You may raise brand recognition and visibility by using off-page SEO techniques like press releases and guest blogging to have your brand recognized on other websites.

4. Increased referral traffic: You may increase referral traffic to your website by using off-page SEO strategies, such as social media marketing and link building. This traffic originates from a variety of outside sources, which may increase audience reach and conversion rates.

A Few Guidelines for Successful On-Page and Off-Page Search Engine Optimization:

Include relevant keywords in the page titles and body tags on all of your material. This may make it simpler for search engines to understand the topic of your website and for customers to find you when they are looking for a certain item or service.

To make it easy for search engine spiders to navigate and examine every page on your website, create a sitemap that lists every page in a logical order.

Improve your images by adding alt text so that viewers and search engines can comprehend the substance of the picture without having to open or analyze it. Make use of social media sites: Facebook, LinkedIn, Twitter, and so on. You may build a presence for your brand and drive more visitors to your website from these channels by regularly publishing interesting content about your business.

Engage in consistent link-building activities to increase your website's authority and exposure in search engine results pages (SERPs). Among them are things like directory uploads and guest blogging.

Keeping Up in the SEO Competition: Strategies and Tactics for Constant Success:

1. Mobile Optimization: A website that is optimized for mobile devices is a must, particularly with the increase in the use of tablets and smartphones. Search engines like Google prioritize websites that are responsive for mobile devices in their search results. If you want to stay ahead of the competition, make sure your website is responsive and offers a seamless user experience across different screen sizes

2. Featured Snippets and Voice Search: The emergence of voice search technology and the growing popularity of devices like Google Home and Amazon Echo have significantly altered peoples' ways of discovering information. Optimizing your content for highlighted snippets might help you get more visibility and rank higher in search results. Consider how your content is structured and written in a conversational tone to match the way that people pose inquiries.

3.The user experience has a significant impact on search engine results, along with fundamental web elements. Pay attention to fundamental online requirements such as speedy page loads, ease of use, and compatibility for mobile devices. To lower bounce rates and boost engagement, enhance the user experience on your website.

4. High-quality and Relevant Content: Content is an essential part of SEO. All the same, search engines are becoming better at figuring out what content is relevant and contextual. Aim to provide top-notch, educational, and engaging content that aligns with the user's objectives. Do a thorough examination of your target keywords to find related topics, then logically incorporate them into your writing.

5. Establishing the three attributes of expertise, authority, and trustworthiness (E.A.T.) in your field is crucial to SEO success. Provide guest articles to respectable magazines, build high-quality backlinks from trustworthy and relevant websites, and showcase happy client testimonials. Search engines will thus see your website as having more legitimacy and authority.

6. Integration of SEO and Social Media: The significance of social media signals for SEO is growing. To encourage engagement and broaden the reach of your content, develop a solid social media strategy. Use social networking sites like Facebook, Instagram, LinkedIn, Twitter, and Facebook to share and encourage people to participate with your most current blog entries, infographics, and videos.

7. Video Content Optimization: A growing number of consumers are beginning to favor viewing videos while absorbing content. Create informative, excellent videos and make sure they are optimized for search engines. Transcribing movies and adding relevant keywords to the titles, descriptions, and tags can help them rank higher in search results.

Local search engine optimization, along with Google My Business, is essential for businesses who have physical locations. Verify and update all the information on your Google My Business page, take control of your listing, and invite customers to write reviews. Your company's chances of appearing in Google Maps local search results will rise as a consequence.

If marketers want to maintain their lead in the SEO competition, they must remain vigilant, embrace new methods, and adapt to emerging patterns. Keep a watch out for updates to search engine algorithms, stay up on industry developments, and regularly review and tweak your SEO tactics. Staying ahead of the competition will help you increase website visibility, attract organic visitors, and achieve long-term success in the digital realm.

Chapter 9: Optimizing Social Media Promotion's Impact

Businesses now advertise their products and services differently thanks to social media. Businesses now have an incredible tool for directly and worldwide reaching out to their target audience, thanks to the rise of social media platforms like Facebook, Instagram, Twitter, and LinkedIn. Businesses of all sizes may benefit in a variety of ways from using social media marketing to your advantage. Some crucial things to consider are the following:

1. Increased brand awareness: Companies may bolster their brand presence and grow their audience by using social media. Companies that provide interesting content and take an active role in conversations may build a strong brand presence and become recognized as industry leaders.

2. Cost-effective advertising: Traditionally, advertising has been an expensive undertaking, especially for small companies. All the same, social media marketing offers more affordable alternatives to traditional advertising tactics. By deploying customized advertisements, businesses may reach their intended demographic at a far lower cost.

3. A greater level of customer involvement: Social media platforms provide businesses the chance to communicate directly with

customers, fostering a feeling of community and strengthening bonds. By replying to comments, addressing problems, and providing relevant information, businesses may build long-lasting connections with their customers and encourage brand loyalty.

4. Real-time market research and consumer input: Social media provides businesses with a means of obtaining real-time customer feedback. By listening to their audience, businesses may get information about market trends, comprehend consumer preferences, and make informed decisions.

5. Increased website traffic and lead generation: Social media is an effective technique for bringing prospective customers to businesses' websites. By releasing interesting material and carefully selecting links, businesses may increase website traffic and lead creation. This might result in more revenue and sales.

6. Improved search engine rankings: A social media presence for a business may help it rank higher in search results. A website's rating is increased by search engines when users interact with it and share it on social media, since these signals are seen as genuine and relevant.

It is essential to recognize, however, that a well-thought-out approach is needed for social media marketing to be effective. The following tactics will help you get the most out of social media marketing:

1. Identify your goals: Clearly state your goals for using social media marketing. Having specific goals will direct your social media strategy, whether it is increasing brand awareness, increasing website traffic, or generating leads.

2. Recognize your target audience: Creating content that is both relevant and engaging requires a thorough understanding of your target audience. Examine the activities, interests, and demographics of your audience to modify your message.

3. Produce quality material: When it comes to social media marketing, content is king. Make an investment in producing valuable, shareable content for your audience. These may be podcasts, infographics, videos, or blog posts.

4. Interact with your audience: Success on social media requires establishing rapport and establishing a connection with your audience. To promote a sense of community and increase brand loyalty, reply to comments, address inquiries, and start discussions.

5. Monitor and evaluate your results: Keep a close eye on your social media initiatives and gauge their effectiveness on a regular basis. Track important variables like website traffic, engagement rate, and conversion rates using analytics tools. This will assist you in determining what is effective and what needs improvement.

Creating a Social Media Persona for Your Brand: Methods for Genuine Engagement

Building a solid and real brand identity on social media is essential to engaging with today's consumers in the always changing world of digital marketing. Social media's widespread use in people's lives has given marketers the opportunity to engage in meaningful dialogues in addition to traditional forms of advertising.

1. Establishing Your Brand's Identity:

Defining a distinct and cohesive brand identity is fundamental to building a brand character. This necessitates knowing your brand's values, goal, and vision. Begin by answering these basic queries: What is the essence of your brand? What are the primary principles it adheres to? How is it different? The basis for a genuine brand character that is in line with the essence of your company is laid by using this introspective approach.

2. Uniformity across platforms:

When it comes to social media brand development, consistency is key. Maintaining a consistent voice and visual style on all platforms should be a simple task for your brand persona. A consistent presence establishes familiarity and trust with your audience, from the tone of your posts to the colors and design elements. Maintaining a consistent brand image throughout social media platforms such as Facebook, Instagram, Twitter, and emerging ones helps to fortify your identification.

3. Putting a Human Face on Your Company:

Humanizing your brand is essential in the digital sphere, where interactions often lack face-to-face contact. This entails introducing the individuals who run the company, such as the executives, staff, and even clients. Share behind-the-scenes photos and videos to give people a glimpse into your company culture. By emphasizing your company's human side, you may establish a meaningful connection with your audience and dissolve the boundaries that separate them from your brand.

4. Having an authentic conversation:

Genuine conversations on social media are based on authenticity. Respond to messages, mentions, and comments to engage your audience in active communication. Genuine interactions are necessary for authentic engagement; automated replies are not enough.Spend some time learning about the problems that your audience is facing, answering their questions, and expressing your appreciation for their support. Positive brand impression is influenced by these personal ties.

5.Using Stories to Create an Emotional Connection: Using stories to create an emotional connection with your audience is a terrific strategy. Provide narratives that depict the development of your brand, the challenges faced, and the successes achieved. Your target audience should be able to relate to these tales and feel things that are consistent with your business's ideals. Think about displaying actual customer experiences with your goods or services via user-generated content. A feeling of belonging and community is fostered by authentic storytelling.

Social Media Marketing's Significance for Your bus*iness*

These days, having a strong social media presence is essential for brands—it is not simply a choice. Social media platform marketing has grown significantly in the last few years.

Innovative functionalities such as Facebook's live feature and SnapChat's ephemeral content are enabling brands to engage with their audience more efficiently.

These days, a strong social media presence is essential for your business for the following seven reasons:

1. search engine exposure

All businesses want to increase traffic and user interaction, but can they do this if potential customers cannot find you online? Your ability to control the first search result page in a more organic way with social media accounts increases sales. Millennials' value will increase since they spend a significant amount of time on social media.Additionally, being active on social media can help you not only attract business but also overcome bad brand perception in order to rank well.

You have the opportunity to create narrative via online social networking to draw in customers. Every tweet and Facebook post has the potential to disclose a company's ethics, ideals, and much more. However, avoid sending N or more updates every day to your followers. Verify whether anything is relevant.

2. Channels for Developing Faith

Nowadays, having a social media presence is essential to winning over customers. It's OK to exist without a physical business, but it will be looked down upon if you don't interact with people. This holds true for all internet-based businesses, whether they are startups or online stores. You are losing out on brand-important profiles if you are not engaged on social media.

3. A Point of Advantage in Competition

Do you think the people that compete with you also don't give a damn about their social media presence? It's possible you're off. There is a good chance that they are spending time and money to establish a reputable social media presence in order to attract clients. You will lose out on all the advantages of social media presence and your competitor will gain an advantage over you. Take a close look around to discover what they have been up to.

4. Online Customer Connect

For internet businesses, gaining clients' trust and proving their legitimacy are essential. You have the opportunity to build relationships with your clients via social networking sites. Using a variety of social media platforms to promote your services is something that brands must understand is essential in order to keep customers interested. As an example, you may communicate with customers and provide them a chance to participate with your company via creative Facebook posts.

5. Company Leads & Sales

One of the best ways to get leads is via social networking. Social media's impact has increased further with the emergence of new platforms like YouTube and Pinterest that enable direct sales. In order to facilitate audience shopping and program installation, Instagram also included a call to action button. The rapidly changing social media landscape will soon significantly impact sales. Furthermore, you will be the losing party if you are not there when it occurs.

6. Avenues of Marketing

One of social networking sites' primary benefits is said to be boosting sales. With the purpose of helping marketers engage with their target audience, all social media networks have established marketing infrastructure. Two of the most well-liked channels for advertising goods and services are Twitter's marketing campaigns and Facebook's sponsored posts.Distinct marketing channels are available on every social media platform. Having a social media presence will increase the benefits even if it's not a must to utilize these sites. International businesses use social media links to drive followers and likes for their marketing initiatives.When used properly, social media may have a huge impact on your organization and lead to success. It makes no sense to avoid utilizing social media because of the quantifiable benefits it offers.

Chapter 10: Types of Content to Post on Social Media

1. Blog Posts

Not only are blog articles a terrific method to increase traffic to your website, create thought leadership, help your customers, and more, but they are also one of the most prevalent pieces of material to publish on social media.

Social networking can be a great avenue to promote new blog entries when they are published, re-market old content that is still relevant, and attract new customers. Valuable blog postings are instructive, useful, interesting, etc. Sharing these on social media helps your potential consumers and can help promote your business too.

2. Website Resources

To draw more attention to your website's resources, boost traffic, and even generate leads for your business, you may share them on social media in addition to posting blog material. Content like podcasts, presentation decks, eBooks, white papers, case studies, and more could be useful to your prospective clients. Any materials you have that your target audience would find useful might be promoted on social media.

3. References

Testimonials are another kind of content to share on social media and may be used as a kind of social proof on your website. Although they lean more toward being promotional than instructive, they are nonetheless important and engaging for the people who are intended to read them.

Social networking is a great place to post endorsements, reviews, and general good feedback from your existing customers. In addition to being essential trust signals for your website, displaying them on social media gives you the chance to stand out, advertise to your present clientele, and attract new ones.

4. Selected Information

The goal of social media is to foster community development and communication. It is not enough to constantly market oneself; you also need to give back to society. One of the biggest mistakes businesses make with social media marketing is promoting too much and focusing too little on providing value, listening, and communicating.

Use a more strategic approach that works for your business, your target market, and their social media use habits rather than just advertising all the time. For a more well-rounded and community-focused feed, include a variety of interesting, entertaining, uplifting, and educational content that your audience will like.

Sharing or selecting useful material from other sources might fall under this category. Reshare articles written by influential people in your industry, interesting posts from other sites, information from alliances your company has built, amusing memes, and much more. Just be careful to provide due credit to the original source of any material you gather and distribute.

5. Figures and Data

When creating content for social media promotion, statistics and figures may be helpful tools for your company. An intriguing fact or piece of data may easily be transformed into a lovely, straightforward social media visual.

In addition, a wide range of information is available. You may limit yourself to information and figures directly related to your industry. Moving to a related business or just having a conversation on an intriguing topic related to the environment, animals, etc. are other options.

It can work if it aligns with the interests of your target market and your brand. Posting statistics and information on social media is a terrific idea for organizations, since it raises awareness and education about issues that are so important to charity goals.

6. Pointers

You may also experiment with tips as a great kind of content for your social media marketing. A suggestion may benefit your target audience as well as produce an interesting visual for social media. For this reason, well-crafted recommendations may spark a lot of conversation on your page and help you expand your audience by encouraging reshares of the content.

Additionally, you could learn more about your target audience's social media use habits and top resources by defining them on the platform. This lets you discuss with them the things that they value most and provide suggestions that they are more likely to find beneficial.

7. Verses

Quotes are another kind of material that may easily be turned into a picture, making them a viable option for social media publication. The kinds of quotations that resonate most with individuals will vary depending on who your target audience is. A quote graphic may be a great way to add some visual appeal and diversity to your social media feeds, regardless of whether your audience is drawn to motivating, inspirational, humorous, etc. quotations.

8. Video

Particularly for social media, videos are often a very engaging kind of content. Moreover, this form of material is dynamic and adaptable. Videos on social media might be tutorials, walkthroughs, lengthier films, or shorter pieces. Live video is also a possibility if it makes sense for your company and you can pull it off.

There are Reels and Stories on Instagram. Unlike Stories, which vanish after a day, the Reels feature lets people navigate through movies exclusively and is excellent for small videos you want to stay visible on your page.

Explainer videos and tutorials are helpful to your audience, which may make them a great substitute for posts on social media. One of the best uses of social media marketing for e-commerce is creating product tutorials, but service-based businesses may also benefit greatly from them.

In addition, when you've invested time and energy into making a video, you may use it for a number of purposes to support marketing campaigns that don't revolve around social media. Video material may be repurposed in a variety of ways to support the creation of new content or to advertise other kinds of content on your website and social media channels.

9. Graphics

Infographics are a kind of material that is very visual and works well on social media. Infographics may help break up post types and improve engagement as long as they are well-designed and appealing to your target audience.

10. Announcements from the Company

Social networking might be a great way to communicate news about your company. Once again, you don't want corporate announcements to take up all of your feed. But, it's worthwhile to share a message on social media and celebrate with your loyal customers if something amazing occurred, you reached a milestone, you posted a new position, etc.

11. Highlights of the Product

Highlighting your products on your website or at your retail store is undoubtedly one of the best types of content to share on social media. You may reveal new goods, discuss items that have just gone on sale or clearance, introduce product bundles, highlight limited-edition items that are selling out quickly, and much more.

You may highlight various product qualities in addition to presenting or promoting the product. While product lessons are a great way to use video, you can also use other media to provide further instructions or guidance. You may also draw attention to suggestions or special or advantageous uses for the product.

12. Occurrences

You may use social media to promote events that your company is hosting, sponsoring, or attending, as well as to invite your target audience to attend. If you own a local company, you can also use your social media profiles to help promote events in your community. To help create interest in events that your partners or customers are holding, supporting, or attending, you can also advertise them.

13. Unannounced Looks Behind the Scenes

A glimpse inside the inner workings of your company is another kind of content you should provide on social media. This might include behind-the-scenes looks at a particular step in the manufacturing process, how a product is packaged, and more, all of which highlight the corporate culture of your business.

Your industry and kind of business will determine what "behind the scenes" means for your company. Allowing people to peek behind the scenes might be beneficial for a range of social media networks. It's really one of the creative uses of Instagram Stories for companies.

14. Media Attention

It's critical to share any significant news coverage your business has received on social media. It is technically promotional, but it also includes earned media and carefully chosen content. Additionally, it may help develop brand recognition and thought leadership while enhancing authority within your industry and fostering a sense of trust among prospective clients.

15. Content Created by Users

User-generated content (UGC) is material that is contributed by brand advocates and consumers rather than by your company. User-generated material might include photographs, movies, critiques, and more.

UGC is often gathered via entering contests, using certain hashtags, etc. A UGC campaign or request is often carried out on social media. However, you may cross-post user-generated material on social media if you're running it via your website and have permission to do so.

16. Themes for Holidays

Social media is flooded with holiday stuff. In case your target audience actively celebrates any major holidays, it may be a good idea for your business to provide happy holiday content centered on such occasions.

Social media content with a holiday theme is often happy and amusing. Furthermore, it is advisable to contemplate any particular challenges or barriers that your intended audience could encounter during certain holidays or seasons of the year. Afterward, you may also create holiday material with a stronger business theme to help solve those issues or ease those difficulties.

17. Queries

On social media, questions are a great method to engage your audience and get their response. They also have a tendency to draw engagement. One strategy to improve social media engagement is to pose questions to start discussions.

You may use social media to pose a question to your audience and get a reaction, whether it's lighthearted fun or something more serious for commercial purposes. You could even conduct a survey and share the findings! On social media, you may respond to questions from the public.

If you have FAQs on your website, it's a great place to start for common questions from both new and returning visitors. Reaching out to and helping consumers who have the same question is one approach to provide answers to those on social media. Additionally, you can learn from those interactions and use that feedback to make your responses to those questions even better.

These are just a few examples of social media content types to distribute to get you started on creating your content schedule. While some social media content aims to increase interaction on the platform, other content is designed to direct users to your website.

Chapter 11: Analyzing Transient Media.

Some things aren't meant to last, especially in the field of marketing. Astute entrepreneurs have discovered that, despite its transience, ephemeral content works very well to grab attention.

Examples of ephemeral content include text, videos, and rich media. Such data is intended to disappear after a certain period of time, like a day. Upon the expiration of the designated period, the item becomes unavailable. It disappeared within moments.

There are several social media platforms that provide ephemeral material, including Facebook, Instagram, WhatsApp, Snapchat, and Facebook. All four come with pre-installed choices for temporary content.

Most of the material on Snapchat is temporary. Users may choose with whom to share images or videos with their friends or followers. These postings are removed once 24 hours have passed or after the recipients have seen them twice.

Additionally, individuals may be the authors of the social media narratives that show up on their profiles. The tales may be accessible to the public or the user's followers, depending on the privacy settings of the user.

Instagram and Facebook provide a combination of permanent and transient content. In addition to browsing through their usual feeds, Instagram users may upload photos or videos. In addition, they may compose stories for social media platforms, where they would share them on their profiles before deleting them a day later.

Similar strategy is used by Facebook. Although Facebook allows it, Instagram does not allow sharing text-only material.

Story storage is an option available to users on Facebook and Instagram. The short biography that appears on a person's social network profile is always there (until they delete it).

Although chatting is the primary use case for WhatsApp, there are additional uses for transient material. For example, disappearing messages may disappear after 24, 72, or 90 days. Users can construct their own vanishing messages. Not only that, but they could make short videos to upload to their profiles and gain popularity on social media.

Although ephemeral content has a short shelf life, readers who like a user's messages or stories won't want to miss a fresh addition. Ephemeral alternatives, along with original content, are a useful tool for marketers looking to stand out from the crowd and attract clients.

Benefits of Intermittent Data:

Marketers' knowledge of SEO is useless when it comes to transient content. With ephemeral content, which disappears rapidly, marketers may focus on anything other than long-form, high-ranking material on blogs, videos, or articles.

If they do not check their social media accounts within the given period, users will not see this information in search engine results.

Although ephemeral content's temporary nature may be disappointing, marketers should be aware of some of its key benefits

1.Gen Z and Millennials Appreciate Temporary Data

Do millennials and Gen Z customers make up the majority of your audience? Then, ephemeral content is a must for your social media marketing plan. Increditools reports that Gen Z viewers make up over 70% of Instagram story viewers. Members of the millennial generation make up the bulk of those who continue to watch.

Growing up with fleeting media, Generation Z, the newest generation of millennials, was exposed. Instantly upon its 2011 inception, Snapchat became well-known. After social media giants like Facebook and Instagram started incorporating the ability to share transitory information into their networks, the concept gained popularity between 2011 and 2018.

From 2011 to 2018, Snapchat ranked as the second most popular social networking app among millennials and Generation Z users. Knowing how ever-ephemeral content works, these customers want to see more of their favorite brands and organizations creating it.

Customers' commitment to Snapchat hasn't decreased, despite the fact that fewer people use it than ever before. When it comes to catching up on fleeting material, millennials and Generation Z users often use Instagram and Snapchat.

2. What Your Audience Might See If They Have FOMO

A FOMO is a stand-for "fear of missing out." In order to prevent visitors who choose not to read the post from learning what happened, ephemeral content is only available for a short time. Conversations among their friends or colleagues will remain hidden from them.

Being afraid of missing out is one of the best motivators. It is unpleasant for anybody to be excluded from an activity or to be unaware of any discussions or experiences that other participants may have.

Marketers may benefit from FOMO by creating content that has limited lifespan. Your readers will be more inclined to follow your

story and come back whenever you post anything new if you regularly write succinct, original articles that spark curiosity.

3. It Boosts Audience Brand Engagement

Comments and likes are often left on shared social media content. Should a user find a post particularly fascinating, they may decide to share it with their followers. Viewers are more engaged with the content when post producers may respond to comments. Regular postings, however, may not always include all the interactive narrative elements.

Interactive social media narratives—like surveys and Q&A sections—encourage deeper participation. Businesses may also want to know what their followers think about a certain subject. In response to the story's content, viewers may post short comments, participate in the poll, and answer questions.

One such element of certain ephemeral content is live broadcasting. Exchange items in real time, and let others see what's happening by watching the user's stream. Live streaming could be useful for noteworthy events like product launches or when you have interesting news to share.

People may sometimes post their temporary material within a certain region on social networking sites or tag other users. One way to get
other users share a post with their followers by tagging them in it. Users may now see that you are referenced thanks to this.

4. You Can Increase Your Audience Reach: Advertisers are always seeking ways to draw in new clients, and ephemeral content—especially on Facebook, Instagram, and Snapchat—is a great way to do this.

Unless the user explicitly sets privacy limits, ephemeral material is almost always released openly. When a story garners a lot of attention, it could get to the top of the social media platform's explore feed and show up in the feeds of certain people without their being direct followers.

Companies do not have to pay for their ephemeral material, unlike social media advertisements. Many times, an ephemeral post might go viral and reach hundreds or thousands of people without costing the firm a single money.

Companies with tight advertising expenditures find tales appealing because of this quality. Rather of using sponsored advertisements, companies might create captivating short-lived content and hope for success.

Social media stories are automatically included to certain networks' public algorithms, such as Facebook and Instagram. Your ephemeral content can be discovered by users who click the Explore button on Instagram. They could follow you if they like watching the video. This aids in your gradual build-up of a following on the website.

5. You'll Establish Closer Bonds With Your Audience

Creating a close connection with the audience is one of the hardest problems for companies. An organization's purpose is to close deals, not to become the greatest friends of customers. Nonetheless, businesses who are able to build relationships with their clients are probably going to see higher retention rates.

When a customer perceives that a business really values them and offers exclusive products or services, they will patronize that brand again in the future.

Establishing customer connections via social media is very effective, especially when using ephemeral content. You will probably get more replies from the audience for ephemeral content than you would from standard postings because of its characteristics that encourage audience interaction.

6. Effortlessness Is the GoalThe raw quality of transient material is one of its main advantages. Audiences do not expect professionally created and edited social media content.

Indeed, the more authentic your content seems, the more probable it is to strike a chord with readers. When companies don't go above and beyond to close deals, consumers enjoy it. They are curious about what occurs behind closed doors.

You may showcase the CEO working hard on a new project or share a few office moments with your audience by using the organic nature of an ephemeral post. If you are a restaurant owner, post a few videos of your chef preparing one of your favorite dishes.

Utilizing ephemeral stuff is extremely flexible. It's really one of the most flexible options out there for company promotion.

Take a look at some of the lately trending transient postings. Nike, for example, has a reputation for using Instagram stories to debut their newest shoe designs. Every time Nike releases a new shoe, it usually releases a brand-new story as well. This is a great way for Nike to share the current models with the public.

The mere fact that Nike has a sizable global following of people who like its goods is enough to drive millions of views to some of these posts. But Nike doesn't write the scripts for its tales; the production value is minimal. Alternatively, it may be as easy as someone wearing the newest shoes to introduce the product.

The Consequences of Transient Content:

Social Media is spelled out using Scrabble tiles on the Facebook launch page.Although ephemeral material undoubtedly provides many benefits, there are some drawbacks. Social media posts that vanish won't be advantageous for every business.

The following are some drawbacks to be mindful of:

1. Individuals Will Easily Forget About Your Posts

Ephemeral information is often forgotten due to its transient nature. After reading the tale once or twice, users are often unable to see it again. Customers may quickly forget about your business if your message is uninteresting and blends in with the millions of other social media stories.

Because of this, it's advisable to avoid depending on transient updates for important details you want the public to be aware of regarding your company. For instance, you wouldn't provide your company's address or phone number in an ephemeral post. Those are timeless information that need to be available to everybody who requests them.

You will most likely need to adhere to a rigorous publishing schedule in order to get the most out of your ephemeral material. To keep your audience interested, you may need to provide content every day. That may take a lot of time, especially if your marketing budget is tight.

Of course, a number of services allow you to save transient material. You may save an amazing Instagram story as a highlight on your profile if you want others to be able to see it for longer than 24 hours. Whoever pulls it up will be able to access it. But because it's not as fresh, you may not see nearly as much interaction with it.

2. You Can Only Find Ephemeral Content on Social Media

At the moment, only social networking sites save transient content. Ephemeral material cannot be created for whitepapers, blog posts, or other marketing purposes. Since they are meant to be seen for an extended period of time, they will stay visible on your website and in search engine results until you remove them.

Although it is theoretically possible to publish a blog post one day and remove it the next, this is often not a wise move. As blogs gain popularity and rank higher in search results, they usually get more attention over time. A blog that is posted and taken down quickly will never get any momentum. You may send someone an email with it, but if they don't act right away, it will disappear.

Some businesses learn that social media isn't the best place to promote their goods or services. Even if they have an account, they probably don't have many followers, so creating fleeting content won't bring in much money.

A podiatrist, for example, would presumably not want to make fleeting social media updates. Although the treatment they do may

help people with foot problems, viewers are unlikely to want pictures of bunions or toenails all over their Instagram accounts.

Podiatrists also have to follow rules like HIPAA, which require them to be very careful with their patients' privacy. If they have any social media profiles at all, they must exercise extreme caution in what they post there.

3. You Must Formulate a Long-Term Plan

Like with other forms of marketing, you'll need a long-term plan if you want to employ ephemeral content as the cornerstone of your brand promotion. That may consume up a significant amount of your resources, particularly if you have a tight budget and few employees who can work on it in-house.

The majority of businesses learn that they must monitor their fleeting postings all week long. If not, social media algorithms will stop finding their material interesting and their pieces will not rank as highly. You'll need to have a ton of material to fill up your regular posts and be prepared to create them.

Although creating ephemeral material requires less preparation than creating a written piece, sponsored advertisement, or commercial, it doesn't mean you can publish whatever you want. They may quit viewing your stories and unfollow your company if your content doesn't regularly captivate your audience. Nobody likes to waste their limited time on activities that make them feel bored.

The Best Methods for Producing Transient Content:

A man affixing paper sheets to the wall using a board

If you've determined that ephemeral material is appropriate for your brand, try to adhere to these guidelines.

1. Clearly state your goals and create a plan.

What do you want to achieve with your transient content? Are you trying to get conversions, such as email subscription sign-ups, or just brand awareness? Is increasing sales what you're after?

After you've determined what your objectives are, you can choose the kinds of postings that will help you reach them.

For instance, if you want to increase sales, you might use your ephemeral posts to inform your followers about daily promotions on certain products on your online store. People will follow you and often check your stories to see if there are any deals on items they need once they are aware of what you have to offer.

Additionally, you must choose a posting schedule. Do you think a weekly share would be more appropriate, or are daily postings okay? Increasing your frequency will surely get you more followers, but it might also exhaust you. It's difficult to come up with something fresh every day.

2. Create Interesting Content

Even if the majority of ephemeral material isn't prewritten, you should nonetheless state the post's goal and message. Things that are meaningless and ephemeral are unlikely to attract much attention.

Consider the lessons you want your audience to take away from your writing. For example, you might create a "behind the scenes" post to showcase your staff members while they are working on a major project. It could pique the curiosity of potential candidates who are considering employment with your company. This would be an amazing way to notify your audience about upcoming positions if you want to hire in the near future.

Choose how long to write your article and what you'll write in that period. It is best not to split apart haphazard clips that don't adhere to a set format. Rather, weave them into a coherent narrative.

3. Decide If Labels Should Be Used

You may be able to contact more people using tags, even if they aren't huge supporters of your company. Your post could appear in a search for the tag, which might lead to more people following you. You may utilize hashtags, which are brief sentences that appear before the hashtag symbol, to reach a wider audience.

You may also use tags to highlight certain individuals, locations, or businesses. For instance, you might include their handles if your material includes a lot of individuals so that their followers would see the post. Similarly, if you work with a firm on your article, it's a wonderful idea to tag them in the finished output.

4. Tell the truth

Ephemeral information isn't meant to be visually appealing or sold. You can alter it and apply a filter, but you don't have to go wild to make it seem better. Remember that your content will only be available for a brief period of time and that you probably won't repeat it. The planet doesn't have to pay for its creation.

Make sure the material reflects your brand's message and values. It must be consistent with the other kinds of material you provide.

If you operated a hair shop, for example, you wouldn't generally include brief details about a local auto show. It wouldn't be indicative of what your company provides. As an alternative, you might provide clients before and after pictures, recommendations for hair products, and details about forthcoming occasions or specials.

Readers are more likely to like your posts if you are devoted to your brand. Once you accept your honesty, you'll start to notice the type of interaction you're seeking for.

Ephemeral Content Has the Potential to Increase Brand Awareness

While ephemeral material has pros and cons, one thing is certain: it may help with international brand communication. People like viewing interesting and compelling ephemeral posts since they are easy to read, even if the content isn't available forever.

Excellent short articles also have the potential to go viral and bring thousands of strangers to your website who would not have otherwise visited.

Establish your objectives and strategy before you start thinking about ephemeral content for your brand. Once you have a plan in place, you can produce engaging, short-lived content for readers.

Chapter 12: What does a key performance indicator (kpi) stand for?

KPIs, or key performance indicators, are quantitative measures of how successfully a business achieves its objectives. Financial indicators and customer happiness are only two of the ways in which KPIs may be used to evaluate a business's performance. A kpi is often used to pinpoint areas in need of improvement and track progress over time with the use of a checklist. KPIs that are often used include revenue growth, customer retention rates, cost of acquisition, website traffic, and employee productivity.

It's critical to routinely review kpis using a kpi checklist in order to stay on top of things and identify issues that need quick action. To make sure the KPIs are trending appropriately, use a KPI checklist to establish goals for each KPI. Consequently, companies are able to monitor these KPIs and use the information to help them make better choices. Along with improved client retention, businesses gain from higher overall performance, profitability, and customer happiness.

Why do kpis matter?

Businesses need to monitor and measure KPIs in order to comprehend how they are doing. It is hard to evaluate projects' performance or gauge progress without this information. But with the right KPIs in place, you can decide how to take your business and

pinpoint areas that need development. KPIs are crucial for several reasons.
 The following are some significant benefits of kpis:

1.Gives clarity and concentration.

KPIs assist companies in defining success and maintaining focus on their most crucial goals. They establish priorities and distribute funds appropriately. Employees are more likely to remain motivated and focused on reaching their objectives when they are all aware of the KPIs they are aiming for inside the company.

2.Motivates conduct and responsibility

KPIs make teams responsible for their output. When people are given explicit KPIs, they know exactly what is expected of them and what they must do to achieve. This guarantees that everyone is working toward the same objectives and influences behavior.

3.Makes Data-Driven Judgments Possible

KPIs provide an approach to track advancement and evaluate performance over time. They facilitate the process of creating data-driven judgments by providing unbiased, quantitative data that can be used to recognize patterns and arrive at well-informed conclusions. This aids businesses in better resource allocation, forecasting, and pinpointing areas in need of development.

4.Encourages Constant Progress

KPIs aid in identifying areas in need of development and establishing success criteria. This enables companies to keep an eye on their performance and make necessary adjustments over time to guarantee that they consistently strive toward their objectives. Organizations may encourage a continuous improvement culture and make sure they are always trying to become better by establishing kpis.

For firms to make data-driven choices, hold themselves responsible, remain goal-focused, and continually improve performance, they are essential.

5.Encourages Constant Improvement

KPIs aid in identifying areas in need of development and establishing success criteria. This enables companies to keep an eye on their performance and make necessary adjustments over time to guarantee that they consistently strive toward their objectives. Organizations may encourage a continuous improvement culture and make sure they are always trying to become better by establishing kpis.

For firms to make data-driven choices, hold themselves responsible, remain goal-focused, and continually improve performance, they are essential.

What Is The Difference Between Kpis and Metrics?

While both kpis and metrics are used to monitor performance, they have distinct uses and attributes.

Quantifiable data items that provide light on certain performance areas are called metrics. They may be tracked over time and are quantifiable. Although metrics usually lack a defined purpose or goal, they may be used to examine historical performance and spot patterns.

On the other hand, kpis are particular performance indicators that are linked to a target or aim. They gauge the advancement of certain goals and are often connected to essential elements of success.

KPIs provide a means of gauging an entity's or a person's performance in reaching certain objectives. KPIs ensure that everyone is pursuing the same goals and that progress can be tracked regularly and effectively.

KPIs and metrics both give information about performance. Metrics are often used for trend analysis and performance analysis. KPIs, on the other hand, establish a defined target or goal to strive toward and track progress toward specified goals.

The Difference Between Kpi, Goal, and Target:

Now that you know the difference between metric and kpi, how about the other units? Even though the terms goal, target, and kpi are sometimes used synonymously, they have distinct meanings in corporate performance management. It is better to think of these three as separate but connected components than as a singularity.

As you may already be aware, a key performance indicator, or KPI, is a measurable statistic that is used to evaluate how successfully a company accomplishes its primary objectives. It shows how things have changed over time and highlights areas that still need improvement. With the help of KPIs, teams can make data-driven decisions and maintain focus on what actually matters.

A target is a specific, measurable objective that an organization intends to reach within a certain timeframe. It often establishes exact achievement requirements by collaborating with KPIs. Objectives should be aligned with the organization's goals and should be both reachable and aspirational. The team has a direction to follow after KPI targets are established.

The longer-term, more broad goals that a corporation hopes to achieve are called aim goals. The company's overall direction and vision are established by them, along with a variety of objectives and KPIs. The broad picture of an organization's intended results is provided by its objectives.

Numerous KPI (key performance indicator) kinds are available in a variety of sizes and shapes, depending upon your specific needs. Certain Key Performance Indicators (KPIs) focus on customer satisfaction, while others evaluate the success of marketing campaigns. However, they are all included in the following groups:

5. Encourages Constant Improvement

KPIs aid in identifying areas in need of development and establishing success criteria. This enables companies to keep an eye on their performance and make necessary adjustments over time to guarantee that they consistently strive toward their objectives. Organizations may encourage a continuous improvement culture and make sure they are always trying to become better by establishing kpis.

For firms to make data-driven choices, hold themselves responsible, remain goal-focused, and continually improve performance, they are essential.

What Is The Difference Between Kpis and Metrics?

While both kpis and metrics are used to monitor performance, they have distinct uses and attributes.

Quantifiable data items that provide light on certain performance areas are called metrics. They may be tracked over time and are quantifiable. Although metrics usually lack a defined purpose or goal, they may be used to examine historical performance and spot patterns.

On the other hand, kpis are particular performance indicators that are linked to a target or aim. They gauge the advancement of certain goals and are often connected to essential elements of success.

KPIs provide a means of gauging an entity's or a person's performance in reaching certain objectives. KPIs ensure that everyone is pursuing the same goals and that progress can be tracked regularly and effectively.

KPIs and metrics both give information about performance. Metrics are often used for trend analysis and performance analysis. KPIs, on the other hand, establish a defined target or goal to strive toward and track progress toward specified goals.

The Difference Between Kpi, Goal, and Target:

Now that you know the difference between metric and kpi, how about the other units? Even though the terms goal, target, and kpi are sometimes used synonymously, they have distinct meanings in corporate performance management.

It is better to think of these three as separate but connected components than as a singularity.

As you may already be aware, a key performance indicator, or KPI, is a measurable statistic that is used to evaluate how successfully a company accomplishes its primary objectives. It shows how things have changed over time and highlights areas that still need improvement. With the help of KPIs, teams can make data-driven decisions and maintain focus on what actually matters.

A target is a specific, measurable objective that an organization intends to reach within a certain timeframe. It often establishes exact achievement requirements by collaborating with KPIs. Objectives should be aligned with the organization's goals and should be both reachable and aspirational. The team has a direction to follow after KPI targets are established.

The longer-term, more broad goals that a corporation hopes to achieve are called aim goals. The company's overall direction and vision are established by them, along with a variety of objectives and KPIs. The broad picture of an organization's intended results is provided by its objectives.

Numerous KPI (key performance indicator) kinds are available in a variety of sizes and shapes, depending upon your specific needs. Certain Key Performance Indicators (KPIs) focus on customer satisfaction, while others evaluate the success of marketing campaigns.

Strategic kpis instances are as follows:

1. Market share

2. Rate of sales increase

3. net profit margin

4. Value of a client for life

5. The ROI (return on investment)

6.KPIs for operations

Metrics known as operational KPIs are used to assess an organization's daily operations and activities. The effectiveness of a company in carrying out its business procedures and achieving its operational goals is tracked by these KPIs. Middle management often uses operational kpis to find opportunities for process optimization and improvement.

Operational kpis examples are as follows:

1. Cost of client acquisition (cac)

2. The rate of turnover

3. The mean revenue per user, or ARPU

4. website visits

5. percentage of on-time deliveries

Functional unit KPIs

Metrics known as functional unit KPIs are used to assess how well certain organizational departments or functions are doing. The performance of each business unit is tracked using these KPIs to make sure it's contributing to the overall success of the company.

Functional unit KPI examples include the following:

1. A customer service department's first-call resolution rate

2. A warehouse or logistics department's inventory turnover

3. the length of time it takes to recruit someone in the HR division

4. A software development team's pace of problem fixes

5.selling a marketing department's qualified leads

Leading vs trailing kpis

Leading KPIs track actions that indicate potential future performance. As an example, a leading kpi for sales performance is the quantity of new leads created. On the other hand, trailing kpis assess the results of previous actions. One trailing kpi for sales performance, for instance, is revenue earned.

Here are some instances of leading vs lagging kpis:

Number of fresh leads produced is ahead; the lead to sales conversion rate is trailing.

Units produced per hour is the leading factor, safety checks performed are the trailing factor, and the quality control rate is the trailing factor.

Frameworks for critical performance indicators

There are a number of well-known KPI frameworks on the list below that may help firms monitor and measure their performance.

control via goals (mbo)

The mbo framework prioritizes the establishment of precise objectives and quantifiable targets in order to enhance the performance of organizations. Within the mbo framework are:

Establishing objectives throughout the company.

Bringing them into line with the general plan of the company.

Evaluating performance based on such objectives.

One meaningful metric (omtm)

A kpi framework called omtm places emphasis on determining the one measure that adds the most value to a business. Organizations who want to concentrate their efforts and concentrate on a limited set of objectives may find this framework useful.

Goals and major outcomes (okr)

Tech businesses often employ the okr goal-setting framework. Setting specific goals, determining the essential outcomes required to meet those goals, and monitoring progress toward those outcomes are all part of this framework. Setting lofty, aspirational objectives and routinely assessing your progress toward them are key components of the Okr framework.

A balanced scorecard

Tracking several indicators from four perspectives—financial, customer, internal processes, and learning and growth—is part of the balanced scorecard, a knowledge process improvement methodology. By balancing financial and non-financial metrics that are important

for long-term success, this framework offers a comprehensive picture of an organization's performance.

How are successful KPIs set?

Establishing specific, quantifiable objectives is essential to long-term success. In this manner, your company can monitor development and pinpoint areas for improvement. Having said that, use these guidelines to create efficient KPIs:

Step 1: ascertain the goal of KPIs.

It's critical to comprehend the purpose of kpis before establishing them. ascertain the precise issues or chances that the company wants to use KPIs to resolve. This will provide the framework for establishing meaningful and purposeful KPIs that are in line with the goals of the company.

Step 2: Establish a strong connection between them and the organization's strategic goals and objectives. Verify that each KPI is quantifiable, relevant to the goal being pursued, and helps to achieve a particular strategic aim.

Step 3: Create sensible KPIs

KPIs need to be intelligent, precise, quantifiable, realistic, relevant, and time-bound. This implies that every KPI needs to be precisely defined, measurable, achievable, significant, and accompanied by a clear roadmap for completion. By using this framework, kpis are made sure to be understandable, practical, and in line with company objectives.

Step4: Verify that they are understood

Make sure that the definition of KPIs is clear and that everyone is aware of how they are assessed and how they affect the company. Confusion, subpar work, and employee disengagement might arise from unclear communication.

Step 5: Iterate as necessary

KPIs are subject to change and should not be considered final. Make that kpis are continually relevant, quantifiable, and help achieve strategic goals by evaluating them on a frequent basis.

Step 6: Avoid kpi overload

An excessive number of KPIs might cause one to get distracted and lessen the importance of each KPI. Consequently, it is advised to restrict the number of KPIs monitored for every strategic goal in order to prevent overload and preserve attention.

The Value of Business Strategy and KPIs:

There are several financial KPIs that you should monitor on a daily basis, such cash flow and outstanding revenue. Financial KPIs may be regularly tracked with bespoke dashboards and alerts if your company uses ERP software.

Your company should monitor KPIs in a number of areas, including operations and sales, in addition to finance. Many businesses make the error of not maintaining consistency in their monitoring throughout many reporting periods and in their goals. KPIs are only helpful to your business if they are regularly monitored for advancement, relevant data is gathered for past performance comparisons, and trends are anticipated.

As an instance

A website that sells goods chooses to use website visits as a key performance indicator. Nevertheless, they don't monitor and give little thought to their conversion rates. The company's internet traffic rose by 320% in the third quarter. But the information gathered is of little value to them since they are not monitoring the conversion rate.

Optimal Techniques

Make sure your KPIs are clear and concise. This will assist you in determining where your organization needs to make significant improvements. Your teams will be more focused on the things that really matter for achieving your company objectives if you carefully choose KPIs that are specific to each department.

Steer clear of picking out gaudy KPIs and forcing them on every team member. By doing this, objectives may become ambiguous or implausible. Furthermore, just because a certain KPI was successful for one industry does not guarantee that it would be as beneficial for another. KPIs differ across sectors and are specific to the business.

Start with a few easy-to-track indications, ideally. To guarantee that your goals are achieved, for instance, choose ten KPI indicators from throughout your organization and assign them to different departments.

Consider Your Business Objectives

Prior to considering KPIs, it is important to establish practical corporate objectives. By establishing realistic objectives, you can assist your teams perform to the best of their abilities and project growth predictions for all indicators.

Firm Size: The size of the company must be taken into account while determining KPIs. Larger organizations may concentrate on long-term growth, acquisition costs, and client lifetime values, whereas smaller companies may concentrate on core values and short-term results.

Every sector, company, and division has a number of departmental KPIs. Your organization could have several divisions, but each one should have its own distinct set of quantitative KPIs.

Teams focused on marketing, for instance, have different objectives than those in sales. Because of this, even if both teams keep an eye on sales data, their KPIs could not match. A marketing department's KPIs

may center on impressions, click-through rates, and increases in website traffic; in contrast, a sales team may be more concerned with acquiring new customers and growing at a faster pace.

Making Use of Management

All areas of a company may benefit from KPIs, but finance teams and decision-makers stand to gain the most from them. Decision-makers are better equipped to make judgments and efficiently monitor performance in real-time when they maintain a close watch on key performance indicators (KPIs) throughout the whole organization, including the financial sector.

KPI Measures Are Beneficial

1.Check in to make sure you are on course to meet your financial objectives.

2.Make use of these important measures to assess the effectiveness of your plan.

3.Ascertain which aspects of your company can benefit from improvement.

4.Analyze the potential advantages and difficulties.

5.Evaluate your consumers' happiness level.

6.Net profit and other financial metrics sample KPIs for each industry.

A company's primary objective is to generate revenue. Companies shouldn't be making more money than they are losing. It is crucial to monitor this key performance indicator (KPI) as it illustrates the difference between your earnings and the amount you pay suppliers. Adhere to your strategy even if your company's profit margin is increasing. On the other hand, if you saw a decline, you would have to adapt.

Both the Arrival and Departure

Flow in and out is one of the most crucial KPIs for small companies. This metric may be used by business owners to determine if their margins and sales are appropriate. It is also useful for paying taxes, making new purchases, and calculating financial surpluses. Either more conventional financial methods or ERP software may be used to monitor this data.

The proportion of Revenue

Profit or sales growth determines a company's revenue. The revenue rate will rise in tandem with an increase in sales or profits for your business. Monitor both past and present revenue growth rates to make sure your business is moving forward as planned.

Gross Inventory Value

The amount of shares that a firm has sold over time may be determined by looking at its stock turnover. ERP software makes it simple to monitor stock profits and losses and manage inventories in real time.

The Rate of Accounts Payable

You need to monitor your rate of account payable to make sure that all of your suppliers are paid. An ERP financial application or other conventional financial tools, such as balance sheets, may be used to evaluate this signal. You may determine if cutting supplier expenditure is necessary to increase the company's future earnings by using this Key Performance Indicator (KPI).

Market Share: A company's performance, competitiveness, and place in the market are all gauged by this KPI. Market share is an important metric for evaluating market competitiveness because it gives managers the ability to evaluate the overall growth or decrease of the market, spot notable patterns in consumer behavior, and evaluate their own market potential and opportunity.

A company's position is eventually strengthened and its competitive advantage is increased as its market share increases. A company with a larger market share has greater purchasing power and is exposed to lower supplier pricing. This is due to their substantial order volumes and solid market reputation.

Customer Lifetime Value (CLV) and Customer Metrics:

CLV enables you to assess the value that a long-term client connection is providing for your company. This KPI also assists in identifying the channel that is bringing in the most business at the most affordable cost.

Cost of Customer Acquisition (CAC)

Because it may assist you in assessing the cost-effectiveness of your marketing activities, CAC is regarded as one of the most significant metrics in e-commerce.

NPS, or net promoter score

One of the greatest methods to predict long-term business success is to track your NPS. Send out quarterly surveys to your customers to find out how likely they are to suggest your business to a friend or family member. This will give you an idea of your NPS score. Establish NPS targets and evaluate client satisfaction across your sales teams once a quarter.

Quantity of Clients

You may learn more about whether or not you are satisfying your consumers' demands by counting the number of new and lost clients. Monitoring your customer rate also aids in project growth estimation and has applications in talent acquisition and human resources.

Employee Turnover Rate (ETR) in People Metrics

Take the number of departing workers and divide it by the average number of employees to get your ETR. If your ETR is high, concentrate on reviewing benefits packages, workplace culture, and training initiatives.

Amount Of Responses To Available Positions:

When a large proportion of competent candidates apply for a position, it indicates that you are making excellent use of your exposure to potential hires. By tracking this measure, your business can make sure the financials associated with human resources are in order.

Worker Contentment

Assessing employee satisfaction via surveys and other indicators is essential for the well-being of your department and business. Contented workers may guarantee an organization's success, boost sales KPIs, and onboard new talent.

Regardless of whether your company is new or well-established, selecting the appropriate KPIs is crucial. Making sure your KPIs are being measured in real-time may be achieved by using revenue performance management software or ERPs. ManoByte may assist your company in using more inbound marketing strategies, as well as strategic software and techniques. Speak with a Business Growth Consultant now to see how we can support your company in achieving its goals.

Conclusion

Mixing digital know-how with smart strategies is the key to growing successfully. It's not just about having info but using it cleverly to run businesses better. This combo sparks new ideas, helps make better choices, and lets companies adjust quickly to changes in the market.

When businesses put together what they know about digital stuff with smart plans, they're not just gathering data. They're making a map for success. This teamwork helps them understand customers better, spot trends, and find new chances to do well. The real power comes from using this knowledge, not just having it.